BPP College
Library & Information Service

Correct *Form*

Debrett's Correct Form
Published by Debrett's Limited
18–20 Hill Rise, Richmond,
Surrey TW10 6UA
United Kingdom

Managing Editor
Elizabeth Wyse

Project Editors
Jo Aitchison
Zoë Gullen
Eleanor Mathieson

Additional text for this edition
Carola Campbell and Gabrielle Mander at six

Proof reading and index by Dawn Dobbins

Design concept and style by Officelab, NYC
Page design by Design 23, London
Still life photography by Victoria Dawe

Publisher Ian Castello-Cortes
Chairman Conrad Free

ISBN 1 870520 88 2 / 978 1 870520 88 1

Printed and bound in Portugal by Avarto, Printer Portuguesa

Visit us at www.debretts.co.uk

Correct Form

DEBRETT'S

Contents

Introduction   9

Digital and Business   10
Emails   12
Text Messages   16
Mobile Phones   18
Teleconferences   19
Business Letters   20
Business Cards   22
Business Stationery   23

Invitations   24
Royal Invitations   26
Official Invitations   28
Private Invitations   32
Wedding Invitations   38

Social Events   46
Table Plans   48
Royal Guests   48
Official Functions   50
Private Functions   52
Guest Lists   54
Place Cards   55
Toasts and Speeches   56
Toasts   56
Speeches   57
Visiting Cards   60
Lists of Names   62

American Usage   64
Titles and Styles   66
Styles by Office   69
Visiting Cards   70
Invitations   70

Forms of Address   76
The Royal Family   78
The Queen   78
Members of the Royal Family   80
The Peerage   82
Duke   84
Marquess   86
Earl   88
Viscount   90
Baron   92
Courtesy Titles and Styles   94
Other Titles and Styles   96
Baronet   96
Knight   98
Dame   102
Privy Counsellor   104
Untitled Persons   105
Joint Forms of Address   106

Contents

Daily Life   108
Letter Writing   110
Births and Ceremonies   112
Engagement   114
Bereavement   116
Thank you letters   118
Greetings Cards   120
Change of Address   121

Orders and Decorations   122
Letters after the Name   124
Orders and Decorations   130

Styles by Office   134
Religion   136
Academics   146
The Armed Forces   148
Diplomatic Service   153
Law   154
Medicine   156
Police   158
Politics   159
Local Government   160

Appendices   164
Tables of Precedence   166
Further Information   170
Credits   180
Index   182

Introduction

For more than a quarter of a century, *Correct Form* has provided guidance on the notoriously complex system of British titles and styles. In many ways, forms of address are now more complicated than they were when more formal rules were applied universally. *Correct Form* takes care to reflect the changes of the modern day.

A big change since the publication of the last edition of *Correct Form* is the expansion of digital technology. This new edition offers fresh guidance on business usage, including teleconferencing, as well as mobile telephones, text messaging and email.

Advice is offered on more general day-to-day topics such as letter writing, thank you letters and greeting cards, along with guidance on important occasions of life such as births, christenings, engagements and bereavement.

There is detailed advice on how to address members of the Royal Family, the Peerage, members of the Church and the Armed Forces, as well as the academic, legal and medical professions, along with more traditional matters such as toasts, speeches and precedence.

The new format features photography, sample letters and quick reference tables, making it easier to use than ever before.

In an increasingly informal world, where traditional communication is being transformed by new technology, *Correct Form* is an indispensable guide to the proper forms of address and their usage.

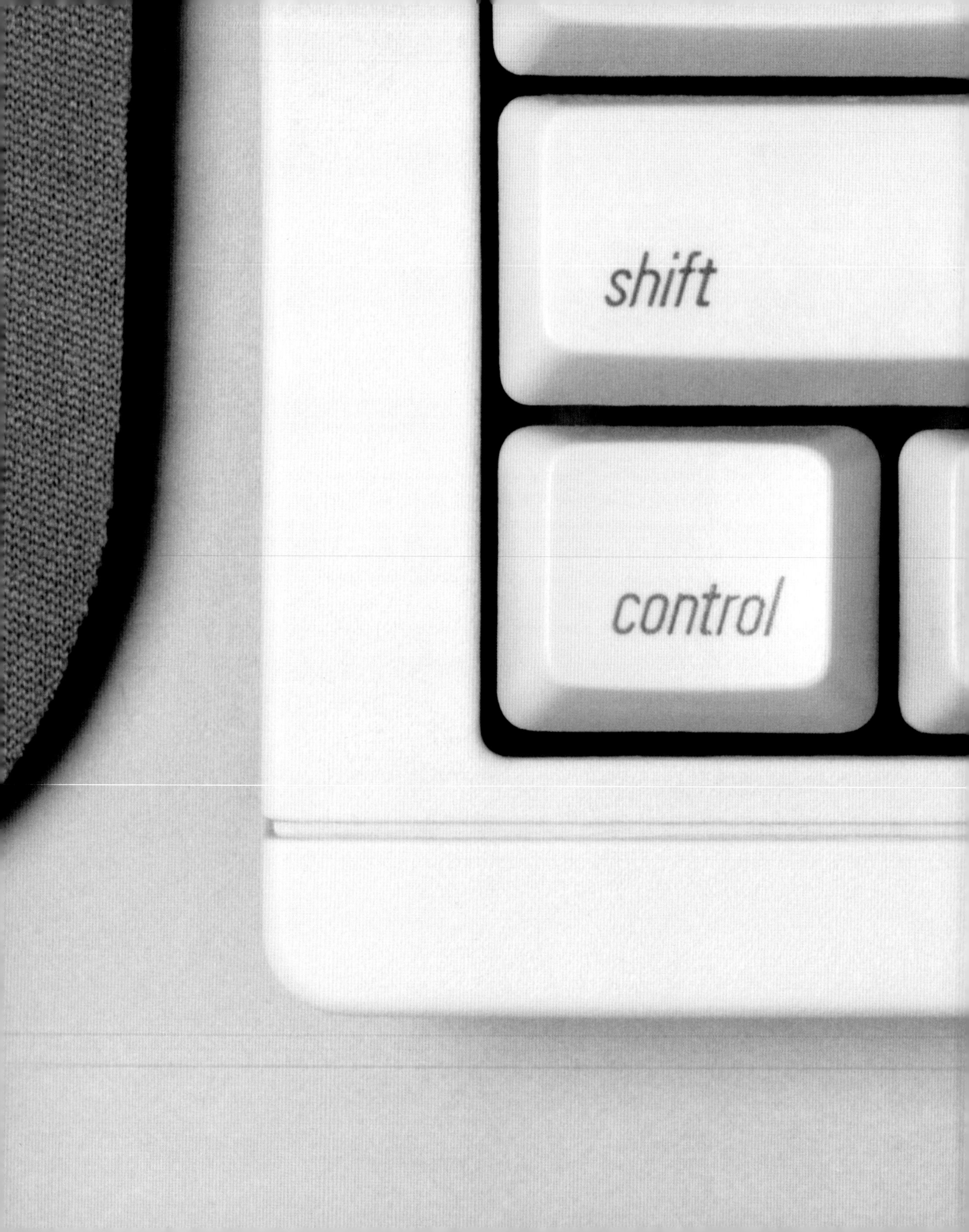
shift
control

Digital &
Business

Emails

Email has replaced many traditional forms of communication, including formal written business correspondence, telephonic conversations between business colleagues, and informal 'chatty' verbal communications.

Email is digital, will be stored forever and can be propagated exponentially. There is, therefore, no such thing as a secure or confidential email. It should not be used for delicate communications or anything that the sender would not want attributed to themselves.

Contents should be kept succinct and non-contentious; avoid email disputes. Curt or angry words look worse when represented digitally.

Nothing replaces real paper and ink; email should therefore not be used for any formal or semi-formal personal correspondence, such as replying to postal invitations, acknowledging births, deaths and marriages, or thank you letters.

If, however, an invitation is received by email, then it is correct to reply by email.

The basic rules of spelling and grammar should be applied to writing an email; it is a written document just like any letter.

SPELLING AND GRAMMAR	Ensure that correct punctuation is used, and do not succumb to the habit of using lower case letters throughout.
FORMATTING	An email is usually viewed both on screen and printed out; the email must therefore look well laid out in both instances. The layout and format of the email should reflect its purpose, i.e. business or social.
RECIPIENTS	Emails should only be sent to those to whom the content is relevant. Avoid bombarding recipients with irrelevant messages. If there is more than one recipient, they should be ordered alphabetically or, in a business environment, by importance.
	When an email is sent in error, the recipient should be contacted immediately by telephone and asked to ignore/delete the message.

DELIVERY AND READ RECEIPTS	Receipts are the digital equivalent of registered post, and can be useful if an email communication is particularly urgent or important. They can be used to confirm that the email has arrived (delivery receipt) or been viewed (read receipt).
THE SUBJECT LINE	The subject line is a summary of the content of the email, and should alert the recipient. A well-written subject line will ensure that the message gets the appropriate attention. It is also used for filing and retrieval purposes so it is important that it accurately reflects the topic of the email.
HIGH IMPORTANCE OR URGENT FLAG	High importance flags – indicating the need for an immediate response – must only be used for genuinely important or urgent messages.
CC AND BCC	Copies ('cc') can be sent to individuals who only need to view the information for reference. Again, they must be ordered correctly. Blind copying ('bcc') should seldom be used; it is deceptive to the primary recipient. Instead, the email should be forwarded on to the third party, with a short note explaining any confidentiality, after its distribution. If blind copying is essential – i.e. for a confidential document where all recipients must remain anonymous – then senders should address the email to themselves, and list all recipients as 'bcc' recipients. The recipients will, therefore, be aware that the full distribution list has been hidden from them.
ATTACHMENTS	Ensure that email attachments are sent in a format that the recipient will be able to read. The recipient should always be alerted to the attachment in the body text of the email. Large attachments, which may exceed the recipient's mailbox capacity, should be sent with caution. Large emails should be broken down into a series of smaller emails whenever possible. Inappropriate images must never be sent as email attachments, especially from a business address.

TELEPHONIC REPLACEMENT	Emails are often used instead of the telephone but, if the message is complex, it should be supported by a phone call or meeting request. Email is therefore used simply to introduce the subject; the writing should be kept clear, simple and to the point. Complex issues and finer details should be discussed face-to-face.
REPLIES	As with letters, it is polite to reply to emails promptly. Just a few words can suffice as a holding reply, and will reassure the sender that the email has actually been received, until a more detailed note can be composed.
	Written correspondence must never be replied to solely by email. If an urgent response is necessary, then a telephone call or email is acceptable, provided it is followed up with the appropriate written correspondence.
	The 'reply' option should only be used when replying to the original email, and if the subject line is still relevant.
	'Reply all' should be used with caution, and only if the entire distribution list needs to be kept up to date on events.
	In the majority of instances, it is preferable to create a completely new message, with its own subject line to avoid including old, trailing emails.
AUTOMATIC SIGNATURES	It is common to have a choice of several different professional and informal signatures. Business email signatures should supply relevant information to the recipient, such as job title, company website address, telephone number and email address.
	They often include a company disclaimer, for example: 'The information in this message is legally privileged and confidential information intended only for the individual or entity named as the recipient....'
TONE	Unlike an interactive telephonic or face-to-face conversation, it is impossible to judge how the recipient will interpret any comments in an email.
	The writing should, therefore, be kept brief, simple and to the point. Any sarcasm or subtle humour must be tempered, especially in messages between those who are less well-acquainted.
	It is wise to err towards the formal. The level of formality/informality introduced by the original email can be mimicked – as can the salutation and sign off.

Informal salutation ——————

Informal sign off ——————

Katy Butler
_____

From: Katy Butler
Sent: 27 September 2006 17:10
To: 'jjones@miltonjones.com'
Subject: Lunch

John,

Apologies for not ringing you yesterday, but I was caught up in a meeting...

Would be great to catch up on new ideas for next year soon. Is lunch next
Tuesday any good for you?

See you soon

K.

Informative subject line ——————

More formal sign off ——————

Katy Butler
_____

From: Katy Butler
Sent: 27 September 2006 17:06
To: 'mdavenport@krm.co.uk'
Subject: Project deadline

Dear Mr Davenport,

I apologise for not telephoning you yesterday. I had a meeting that lasted
for longer than expected.

The deadline for the project has been confirmed as the 14th October. I will
forward you the delivery details and reference numbers once I receive them.

Kind regards

Katy Butler
Debrett's Limited

Text Messages

Texts are a quick and efficient method of communication. They are usually sent from one mobile phone to another. It is also possible to send texts from/to mobiles and landlines, and convert text to digital voice.

Text messaging began as an informal interaction amongst young people; it is now widely accepted in social and business circles.

PURPOSE   Text messages are a perfect vehicle for short, sharp messages, such as: 'Train delayed will be late 4 the meeting', 'Sam and I meeting @ pub, come and join us'.

CAUTION   Messages are usually personal and only intended for the owner of the mobile phone to which they are sent.

Text messages cannot be secured, however, or the distribution limited. They can be stored indefinitely and propagated at whim.

LANGUAGE   In the past, the language of text messaging was based on acronym and abbreviation. While there is an accepted vernacular of abbreviations and codes, predictive text input has largely overtaken the creative text message.

Messages should, therefore, be written with as much conventional grammar, spelling and punctuation as possible to make them instantly understandable for the recipient.

TONE   Texts are constrained by their short length. Their tone is, therefore, informative, concise and slightly curt.

SALUTATIONS   Text messages do not normally have any kind of salutation, unless they are formal, to a senior business colleague or to someone unfamiliar to the sender.

SIGNING OFF   If the recipient will automatically recognise the sender, and they are familiar, then no sign-off is required. If they are less well acquainted, or if the sender is in any doubt that their number will be recognised, a sign off – i.e. 'Thanks, Jessica' – should be included at the end of the text message.

ALERT TONES   There are a number of tones to signal the arrival of a text message; choose a tone that is simple, short and discreet.

RECIPIENTS	Texts should only be sent to those who need to know the news/information they contain, or who need to take action and/or respond. If the text is distributed to multiple phone numbers, it must be relevant to all the recipients. The recipient list should always be carefully checked before any message is sent.
REPLIES	Not all text messages require a reply. If it is necessary to reassure the sender that the message has arrived, an answer should be sent promptly.
DELIVERY STATUS	The mobile service provider will inform the sender of a message delivery failure. Even a message that sends successfully can arrive hours later, particularly if being sent internationally.
IN COMPANY	The general mobile phone rules apply; it is as rude to read or type a text message in company as it is to receive or make a voice call.
QUIET ZONES	'Quiet' zones should be respected by turning the phone off or silencing the ring and keyboard. It may still be possible to read and create text messages without disturbing those around you – this is one advantage text messages have over voice calls.
EMOTION	Capital letters indicate shouting. Texts should never be used to express any strong emotion; angry words look intimidating on screen and, if the message is delayed, can be completely mistimed.
THANK YOUS	Text messages are a quick and easy way to say thank you. They should never take the place of a handwritten letter, but are convenient for quick, informal thank yous between friends.
CIRCULARS	Round robin text messages, with anecdotes and jokes, should only be distributed to individuals with their consent and should not include anything that could offend.
	Employers may view this behaviour as inappropriate use of business mobiles. Socially it is acceptable if done infrequently and without malicious intent.
OTHER PEOPLE'S TEXT MESSAGES	The same rules apply to text messages as to email or paper. It is unacceptable to read a text message sent to another person's mobile phone.
	It is equally unacceptable to send a text from another person's mobile phone, unless specifically given permission. It may also cause confusion to the recipient if the phone number is recognised as belonging to another.

Mobile Phones

An invaluable and widely-used tool of modern communication, mobile phones should be used with discretion and common sense.

PHONE STATUS　　Mobile phones should be switched off in quiet public places, such as libraries or museums, as well as during concerts, plays, films, religious or civic ceremonies, meetings or social gatherings.

Never let phone calls interrupt face-to-face social meetings or personal moments.

RINGTONES　　Ringtones must not be too loud or invasive to others. They should reflect the purpose of the phone; for example, a sensible, subtle and unobtrusive ringtone is appropriate for the office.

ANSWERING AND TALKING　　In situations where receiving calls is unacceptable, but an urgent call is expected, explain the situation to companions.

URGENT CALLS　　Switch the mobile phone to the 'silent' setting (with vibration). When the call comes through, quietly excuse yourself and answer the call in a quiet place, away from other people.

Alternatively, the mobile phone can be given to a receptionist, concierge or secretary to answer and take a message.

VOICEMAIL GREETINGS　　Voicemail should be personalised; it confirms that the caller has the correct number. This can be a standard generic message, but should be updated periodically.

The greeting would normally contain the name of the owner of the mobile phone, along with an invitation for the caller to leave their name, number and a message.

Calls should be returned promptly, or a text message or email sent to acknowledge that the call, and message, has been received.

VOICEMAIL MESSAGES　　A voicemail message should be clear, concise and to the point, including a name, date and time, a short statement of the purpose and whether a return call is necessary. As a general rule, it is best to leave a contact number.

Teleconferences

A teleconference can be conducted both via the telephone – mobile or landline – and voice over the internet.

Teleconferencing is constrained by the lack of facial expressions and body language. It is therefore important to speak distinctly and keep the tone of voice modulated. All attendees should leave a few seconds between the beginning and end of each exchange to allow for any time delay caused by a satellite connection.

THE CHAIR
The person who organised a social conference will normally be the Chair. The Chair leads the meeting, and ensures that the flow of conversation is maintained. Once the session begins, the Chair should move through the agenda at an appropriate pace and keep all attendees on track.

LOCATION
If the teleconference is mostly an audio speech or presentation, it is polite to put the mute button on until the question and answer session at the end.

ATTENDEES
The attendee list should be carefully constructed. Interactive teleconferences should have a limited number of participants; four is ideal, eight the maximum. Attendees who have to leave before the meeting is over should make their apologies at the start. They should quietly disconnect without any disturbance.

REVIEW
The final session of the teleconference should be a quick review and resumé of what has been discussed and agreed, and of the actions to be taken and by whom. At the end, all attendees should go off-line together. It can appear rude if a sub-set continues on with private discussions; but if individuals have been given a specific task during the meeting and this is an opportunity to address the task, it is acceptable.

VIDEO CONFERENCING
The form for video conferencing is very similar to teleconferencing, but with a few modifications. The most popular devices are the traditional dedicated units with large screens and PCs with web cameras. Some telephones also have video capability.

Attendees can see and hear each other; communication therefore includes facial expressions and body language. Participants should limit their body movements. Late arrivals and early leavers at video conferences should acknowledge their arrival and departure. This should be done very quickly and with as little disruption as possible to the meeting. It is not acceptable to answer phone calls or read text messages during the conference.

Business Letters

PAPER	Letters should be printed on A4 paper that features the sender's company logo, postal address, telephone number and email address.
ADDRESS	The recipient's name and address are listed on the top left-hand side of the sheet.
DATE	The date goes underneath the recipient's name and address, on the left-hand side.
SALUTATION	In general, a letter should be headed 'Dear' followed by the recipient's title (Mr, Mrs, Miss) and surname. If the sender is familiar with the recipient, then the letter can be addressed using their first name only, e.g. 'Dear John'. If the sender has already received correspondence from the recipient, then they should mirror how the recipient styled themself previously. If the sender does not know the name of the recipient, then 'Dear Sir/Madam' can be used. The sender should, however, make every effort to find out the recipient's name in order to personalise the letter.
SUBJECT LINE	It is useful to put a subject line at the top of the body of the letter, after the salutation. It provides a reference for sorting, prioritising and filing.
LENGTH	It is advisable to keep business letters concise, to the point and preferably on one side of a sheet of A4 paper.
SIGN OFF	The sign off depends on the salutation. If the letter is addressed to 'Dear Mr Smith', then the sign off would be 'Yours sincerely'. If it is addressed to 'Dear Sir/Madam', then 'Yours faithfully' is correct.
ENCLOSURE	'Encl.' is placed on a line beneath the signature to indicate that an enclosure(s) should be expected.

DEBRETT'S

Mr John Jones
The Jones Partnership
1 Central Street
Cityville AB1 2EF

Date placed under
recipient's address ————————— 22nd September 2006

Debrett's Limited
18 - 20 Hill Rise
Richmond
Surrey TW10 6UA
United Kingdom

Telephone +44 (0)20 8939 2250
Fax +44 (0)20 8939 2251
people@debretts.co.uk
www.debretts.co.uk

Dear Mr Jones,

Clear subject heading —————————————— Re: Company Information

Following our recent telephone call, I enclose some information about Debrett's Limited and details of our upcoming projects.

I hope you find it all of interest and I look forward to hearing your thoughts. I hope we can organise a date for lunch to discuss the opportunity for us to work together in the future.

Please don't hesitate to contact me if you require any further information.

Sign off indicates
named recipient ———————————— Yours sincerely,

Peter Smith

Head of Marketing

Encl.

Registered in England No. 0408448
VAT Registration No. 863 4233 48

Business Cards

These are used for professional or business purposes only, but with the decline of the visiting card they have taken on some of its social functions. Social usage should, however, be infrequent.

Cards are usually printed, but may be engraved if a more imposing impression is thought appropriate.

SIZE

Business cards should be about the same size as a credit card. They should always be able to fit into a card holder or the card section of a wallet.

DESIGN

The particular style, design and detailing, such as the inclusion of a logo, may be a matter of personal taste or may follow a strict corporate policy.

Either way, an effort should be made to design cards in keeping with the type of business concerned.

INFORMATION

The information included should be:

(i)   The employee's name, without any prefixes. For example: John Smith
(ii)   The company's full postal address and website address
(iii)   The company's landline and fax numbers. If preferred, the employee's direct line or mobile telephone number should be included.
(iv)   The employee's email address

LAYOUT

On a standard business card, the name and professional title should be centred, in large characters, above the name of the firm, or below the company logo.

The address, telephone, fax and email information should appear in smaller characters in the bottom left- and right-hand corners, or spread across the bottom of the card.

PUNCTUATION

Punctuation may be included or omitted as desired.

LETTERS AFTER
THE NAME

On a business card that is intended to show the bearer's qualifications, the appropriate professional letters may be suffixed to the name, for example, FRIBA.

Business Stationery

Compliments Slips

Compliments slips are useful when a longer business letter is unnecessary. They are generally used to accompany a package of information, or when the contents are self-explanatory. They should bear the company's postal address and website address, along with telephone and fax numbers. They are the width of a normal sheet of letterhead stationery, but only a third of the length, fitting easily into an envelope.

It is unnecessary to formally top and tail a compliments slip; a briefer salutation and sign-off is acceptable. For example, just the recipient's name as the salutation, and a sign off of 'Regards' or 'Thanks'. It is also unnecessary to include a date.

Faxes

Although email has become a more widespread method of communication, faxes are still used. The first page of the document to be faxed is called the cover sheet.

The cover sheet should include essential information including: the date; the recipient's name, company and fax number; the sender's name, company, telephone number and fax number. There should also be a space for a brief explanatory message.

Sender's fax number for response

The number of pages, including the cover sheet, should be noted

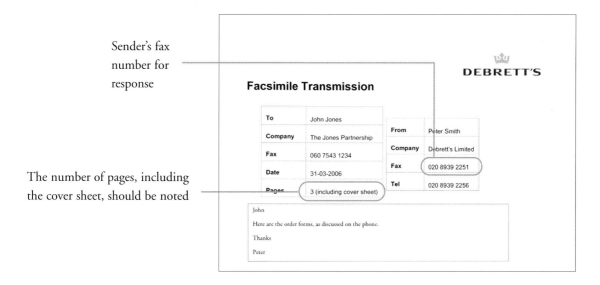

ROBERT &

INVITE YOU TO

ON FRIDAY, 6TH M

AT ST. STEPHEN'S CL

On the Occasion of the Birthday of

Her Majesty Queen Elizabeth II

The British Ambassador

and Wren

request the pleasure of

Mr & Mrs Rupert

Invitations

Royal Invitations

THE SOVEREIGN

Invitations from the Sovereign are sent by:

(i)   The Lord Steward of the Household to a state banquet

(ii) The Lord Chamberlain to all major court functions, such as a garden party, wedding, funeral or memorial service

(iii) The Master of the Household to all domestic functions given by the Sovereign at Buckingham Palace, or where the Sovereign is resident

EXAMPLE WORDING

> The Master of the Household
>
> is Commanded by Her Majesty to invite
>
> Mr and Mrs John Brown
>
> to luncheon at Sandringham House
>
> on Thursday, 10 July at 12.30 o'clock

ACCEPTANCE

All invitations from the Sovereign are commands. Replies should be worded to reflect this and addressed to the member of the Royal Household who has issued the invitation.

NON-ACCEPTANCE

The reason for non-acceptance should always be stated. A prior engagement is not considered to be a sufficient reason for failing to obey the Sovereign's command.

GARDEN PARTIES

An invitation to a garden party is accompanied by an admission card which states that an acknowledgement is not required unless a guest is unable to attend, in which case the admission card must be returned.

A LETTER OF THANKS

When appropriate, such as after a state banquet, but not after a garden party, a letter of thanks is addressed to the member of the Royal Household who forwarded the invitation, asking that thanks are conveyed to the Sovereign.

OTHER MEMBERS OF THE ROYAL FAMILY

Invitations from other members of the Royal Family are not commands. They will usually be forwarded by a member of their Household, to whom the reply should be addressed. In all other respects the invitations are treated as those from the Sovereign.

THE LODGE HOUSE
LANGTON MALTRAVERS
DORSET BH21 0YE
TEL: 01725 843192
FAX: 01725 843193

Reply in the
third person

Mr and Mrs John Brown present their compliments to the Master of the Household, and have the honour to obey Her Majesty's Command to luncheon on 10 July at 12.30 o'clock.

Write out the
time in full

Date at the
bottom of the
letter

23 APRIL 2006

Official Invitations

Invitations to official functions are usually issued on a card, which may be engraved in script from a copper plate or printed in script or Roman type.

It should make clear the following:

(i)   The nature of the function

(ii)   Where the function is to be held

(iii)   The date of the function

(iv)   The time of the function and, if desired, the time at which it is to end

On the Occasion of the Birthday of
Her Majesty Queen Elizabeth II
The British Ambassador
and Lady Wren
request the pleasure of the company of

Mr & Mrs Rupert Bird

at a Reception
on Thursday, 22nd June from 6.00 pm to 9.00 pm
(twilight ceremony between 8 pm and 8.15 pm)

British Embassy

R.S.V.P.
On enclosed card

This card and proof of identity will be requested at the gate

A NOTE ON DRESS	For a function during the day, including a cocktail hour reception, the dress need only be specified if it is to be other than lounge suits: for example, morning dress or academic robes.

For an evening function, dress can be specified: for example, evening dress, dinner jacket or uniform. Decorations should also be specified when appropriate.

ROYAL GUESTS

To indicate that a member of the Royal Family will be present, one of the following is engraved or printed at the top of the card:

> (i) In the gracious presence of Her Majesty The Queen

> (ii) In the presence of His Royal Highness the Prince...

Note: the word 'gracious' is included only for the Sovereign.

INVITATIONS TO ROYAL GUESTS

An invitation to a member of the Royal Family is always extended by letter, either through the Lord-Lieutenant of the county or to the Private Secretary. The latter is the general rule in London, the former elsewhere. A printed invitation is not sent, although a specimen may be forwarded to the Private Secretary if desired.

It may be both prudent and diplomatic to make an informal enquiry, to the Lord-Lieutenant or Private Secretary, as to the possibility of a favourable response prior to extending a formal invitation. The approach should outline the nature and purpose of the function.

Whether the consort of a member of the Royal Family should be included in the invitation depends on the nature of the function. The point can be raised in the informal enquiry.

Only in exceptional circumstances should two or more members of the Royal Family, other than consorts, be invited to the same function. If an invitation to a member of the Royal Family is declined it may subsequently be extended to a more junior member, but never to a more senior one.

Once an invitation to a member of the Royal Family has been accepted, the organisers of the function should discuss with the Private Secretary, or with another member of the Royal Household nominated by him, the detailed arrangements in so far as they concern the royal guest.

HOST AND HOSTESS	Invitations to official functions give the hosts by their office and/or name. This is engraved or printed, with their full title, rank and name followed by decorations.
NAMES ON INVITATIONS	In the case of guests, prefixes such as His Grace and His Excellency are omitted, but The Right Honourable is included for a privy counsellor who is not a peer. The prefix The Honourable and the suffix Esquire are never used. In both cases a man is shown as Mr John Smith.
PAIRS OF GUESTS WHO ARE NOT MARRIED	An invitation to a pair of guests with a relationship other than husband and wife takes one of the following forms: Brother and sister: Mr John Brown and Miss Elizabeth Brown Mother and son: Mrs George Carruthers and Mr William Carruthers Note: invitations to adult offspring are usually sent separately from those to their parents Unmarried couple: Mr Richard Blaine and Miss Ilsa Bond
THE ENVELOPE	An invitation to an official function should be addressed only to the guest invited in their own right if sent to their official address, even if their partner is invited. They are given their full prefix, title, rank and decorations, as for a formal letter. If the invitation is sent to the home address it is traditional for only the wife's name to appear on the envelope.
REPLIES	Replies to invitations are sent on writing paper showing the sender's address. Sample replies are as follows: Mr and Mrs William Brown thank the President and Council of the National Society of… for their kind invitation for Saturday, 12 February, which they accept with much pleasure (or: which they have the honour to accept). Lord and Lady White thank the Master of the Worshipful Company of Clockmakers for his kind invitation for Saturday, 12 February, which they much regret being unable to accept (a reason may be given, for example, owing to a previous engagement, because of absence abroad etc.).

REPLY CARDS	The organisation of a large function is greatly facilitated by the use of reply cards, which should always be printed. The cards are sent out with the invitations and should be of small postcard size.
	Guests should always use the printed card for their reply. Should they wish to add anything, such as an explanation for their inability to accept, this should be done in a separate letter.
ADMISSION CARDS	To assist the toastmaster, or to prevent gatecrashers, the words 'please bring this invitation with you' may be added at the bottom of the invitation card. Alternatively, and especially for an evening function for which a large invitation card cannot easily be carried in a pocket or handbag, the following wording may be added: 'An admission card will be sent on receipt of your acceptance'.
	Admission cards should be printed in Roman type and should not exceed $5^1/_2$ x $3^1/_2$ inches (14 x 9 cm) in size.
	An admission card to a ceremony may be used to allocate a specific seat. To this end, separate admission cards should be sent for a couple, even though they have both been included on the same invitation card.
NAMES ON ADMISSION CARDS	The guest is shown on an admission card by office or by name, in the form in which he or she is to be announced to the host and hostess. If by name, this is limited to title, rank and name, except that the following prefixes should be used:

(i)   'His Grace' for the Archbishops of Canterbury and York

(ii)   'His Eminence' for a cardinal

(iii)   'His [or Her] Excellency' for ambassadors and high commissioners (this may be abbreviated to 'HE' on the card, but not by the announcer)

(iv)   The Right Honourable, the Right Worshipful, the Worshipful etc. for civic heads who are so styled

ENCLOSURES	Additional information or instructions, for example, relating to car parking, are best given on a separate sheet sent with the invitation or with the admission card.

Private Invitations

FORMAL FUNCTIONS

There are two kinds of invitations to formal functions which, unless time is short, are prepared on cards engraved in script from a copperplate:

(i)   Formal luncheon and dinner parties

(ii) At Home invitations for all other parties, such as receptions, garden parties, luncheons, dinners and suppers

INFORMAL FUNCTIONS

Invitations to informal functions may be extended by letter, telephone or email.

It is up to the hosts to decide, and make clear to guests, the appropriate level of formality and all the other relevant details and arrangements. The level of formality of the invitation should accord with that of the occasion.

FORMAL LUNCHEON AND DINNER PARTIES

These are engraved on card of good texture, usually about 6 x $4^1/_2$ inches (15 x 11.5 cm) in size, or slightly larger if necessary. They are prepared in the name of both the host and hostess. If time is short they may be printed, rather than engraved.

The guest's name is handwritten on the top left-hand corner.

Alternatively, the more old-fashioned style of 'request the pleasure of the company of' may be adopted, the guests' names being added on the next line.

If the luncheon or dinner is to take place at an address other than that to which the replies are to be sent – at a hotel, for example – this is stated on a line after the date.

The time may be placed either after the date or at the bottom right-hand corner before, or in place of, the dress code.

STOCK CARDS

Those given to regular formal entertaining may keep a stock of invitation cards. The occasion, date, time and also place, if away from home, are then added by hand.

This card may also be prepared with the wording 'request the pleasure of the company of', the guests' names being added by hand thereafter.

Rupert + Sarah — Use of forename indicates an informal function

Mrs Christopher Wren

at Home
for lunch — Stock At Home invitation with handwritten annotation

on Sunday 8th October at 1 o'clock

R.S.V.P.
Chelsea House
Cheyne Walk
London SW3 5DX

AT HOME
INVITATIONS

At Home invitations for formal occasions are usually engraved on a card of good texture about 6 x 4$^1/_2$ inches (15 x 11.5 cm) in size. This can be slightly larger if necessary. In the case of married couples, these are prepared in the name of the hostess only.

If the time of the function is not a sufficient indication as to its nature, the latter may be stated on the card: for example, 'Dancing 10 o'clock'. If the invitation extends from 6 to 8.30 p.m. the description 'cocktails', 'wine' etc. is unnecessary, though it is often included.

For many At Home functions, with the exception of dances, a smaller card may be used, usually 5$^1/_2$ x 3$^1/_2$ inches (14 x 9 cm), which shows the name of the hostess, At Home, R.S.V.P. and her address. A stock of these cards can be purchased for various functions. Other details are completed by hand.

For small informal parties a basic stock of At Home cards may be purchased, which merely have 'At Home' and 'R.S.V.P.' engraved or printed on them. They would usually be 5$^1/_2$ x 3$^1/_2$ inches (14 x 9 cm). The hostess then adds her name, address, date, time, names of guests and other necessary information.

| **HOST AND HOSTESS** | The exact rank in the peerage of the host and/or hostess is given on all types of invitation. The word 'The' is usually omitted for the ranks of Marquess and Earl, and always for those of Viscount and Baron, as well as their wives. |

No prefixes – such as The Right Honourable, The Honourable or Her Excellency – appear before the name.

No letters are placed after the name.

JOINT HOSTESSES

If there is more than one hostess, their names are placed one after the other. The first name corresponds to the address to which the replies are to be sent.

If a joint party is to be held at a hostess's house and the replies are to be sent to her, her name is placed first on the invitation, irrespective of any title held.

If the hostesses are to deal with replies separately, their addresses are placed from left to right at the foot of the card, in the same order as their names.

OTHER INFORMATION

'Decorations' on a private invitation implies that a member of the Royal Family is expected to be present. Note that the word does not have this meaning on an official invitation.

For functions where the hostess considers it necessary to indicate the dress expected to be worn, 'White Tie' may be added for evening dress, 'Black Tie' for dinner jackets, or 'Afternoon Dress' or 'Informal' for lounge suits.

Otherwise she is content to leave the dress code to the discretion of her guests. Whenever possible, many hostesses will try to indicate more specifically the level of dress expected, either verbally or in a letter if one is being sent with the invitation.

If it is necessary to keep out gatecrashers, 'Please bring this invitation with you' may be added at the foot of the card.

If there is no information to the contrary, it is understood that the function is to be held at the address to which a reply is requested.

If the function takes place in the country, it is useful for a map to be placed on the back of the card or on a separate sheet.

Mr + Mrs Rupert Bird

Guests' names are
handwritten in the
top left-hand corner

Charlotte Pear
invites you to join her
to celebrate
Christopher's 50th birthday

on Thursday, 28th November

at Peardrop Place, London E1

R.S.V.P.
15 Lots Road
London SW10 0QJ
020 7351 5887

Dinner & Dancing
8.00 for 8.30pm
Dress: Drop Dead

Guests should arrive
between these times

Please bring this invitation with you

Rupert + Sarah

ROBERT & JENNIFER

Informal style

INVITE YOU TO DINNER

ON FRIDAY, 6TH MARCH

AT ST. STEPHEN'S CLUB

34 QUEEN ANNE'S GATE, SW1

Replies to the
hostess only

R.S.V.P.
MRS ROBERT BIRD
15 LOTS ROAD
LONDON SW10 0QJ

7.30 PM COCKTAILS
8.00 PM BUFFET DINNER
DRESS: CASUAL

35

SENDING OUT INVITATIONS

It is wise to send invitations as early as possible. While a quiet, intimate dinner among close friends may be arranged over the telephone at short notice, the more formal a gathering, and the more people being invited, the more advisable it is to give advance warning.

Giving notice of a minimum of six weeks before the event should ensure that most people are not already booked up. It will also give guests ample time to reply and provide the hosts with preparation time in abundance.

If an invitation is extended and accepted verbally, for example, by telephone, it should be confirmed by an invitation card on which 'R.S.V.P.' has been deleted and 'To remind' or 'Pour mémoire' substituted. In this case there is no need for acknowledgement.

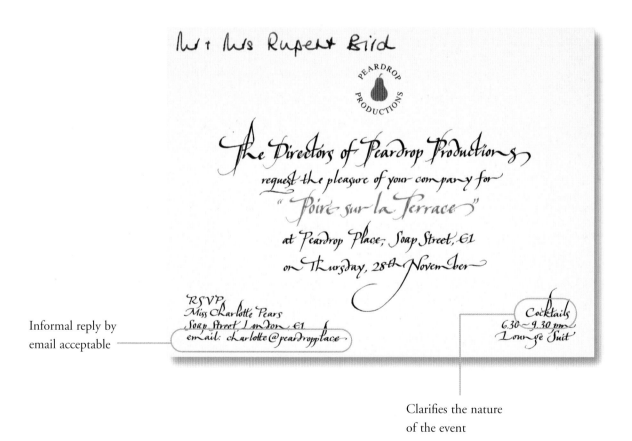

Informal reply by email acceptable

Clarifies the nature of the event

| NAMES OF GUESTS | These are written in the top left corner, except for formal luncheon and dinner invitations designed to include them in the middle of the card. |

The following should be noted:

(i)   No prefixes, such as 'the Right Honourable' or 'the Honourable', are employed

(ii)   No letters after the name are included

All peers and peeresses, apart from dukes and duchesses who are referred to by these titles, are given the form Lord and Lady Blank. This is the established custom for all but the most important private functions, when the exact rank in the peerage may be given.

Grown-up sons and daughters are usually sent separate invitations even when they live at home. However, when their exact names, or their availability, are not known, it is permissible to add 'and Family' after their parents' names.

The addition 'and Guest' or 'and Partner' may be added.

During Ascot week and other similar occasions and festivals for which house parties are given, invitations may show the words 'and House Party' after the names of the guests.

ENVELOPE

It is still customary to address the envelope of an invitation to both husband and wife to the wife only. Guests are given their full prefix, title, rank and decorations, as for a formal letter.

REPLIES

Replies are sent on writing paper with the address, as for official functions. They are addressed to the hostess even when the invitation is a joint one from both the host and hostess.

When invitations are extended to unnamed guests such as 'and Partner' or 'and Family', the reply should contain the names of those who will attend.

A named invitee should be substituted with another guest only if the hostess gives her express permission.

Wedding Invitations

The most traditional and elegant wedding invitations combine quality of material with simplicity of style.

They consist of four pages and are engraved from copperplate on heavy card, usually in black copperplate script on a white or cream matt background.

DIMENSIONS	The usual dimensions are 8 x 6 inches (20.3 x 15.2 cm).
NAMES OF GUESTS	The names of guests are written in the top left-hand corner of the invitation. Names are styled as for official functions, and should be handwritten in an appropriately coloured ink.
DIVORCED PARENTS	There are a number of styles available for the host and hostess, a number of which are listed here. If the bride's parents have married again, the second husband and/or wife do not play a prominent part at the wedding.
INVITATION TO THE RECEPTION ONLY	It is acceptable to invite guests to the reception only. A note should be placed inside the envelope with the invitation to give the reason.
	For example: 'Owing to the small size of Little Wotton Church it is possible to ask only very few guests to the service. We hope you will forgive this invitation being to the reception only.'
	Under no circumstances should a guest be invited to the wedding but not to the reception.
ENCLOSURES	Invitations may come with a variety of enclosures. Some hosts include reply cards.
	It may sometimes be wise to include a map on a separate sheet of paper, as well as any other details, such as transport arrangements.
	If reply cards are to be used, these are usually printed, with a space for guests to fill in their names. They should measure $3\frac{1}{2}$ x $5\frac{1}{2}$ inches (9 x 14 cm).

Mr & Mrs Nicholas Pear

Mr and Mrs Christopher Wren
request the pleasure of
your company at the marriage
of their daughter
Jennifer
to
Mr Robin Bird
at the Church of St. Francis, Chelsea
on Saturday, 1st May 2007
at 3 o'clock
and afterwards at
14 Birdcage Walk, SW1 ——————— The wedding reception

R.S.V.P.   The reply to be
15 Lots Road   addressed to the
London SW10 0QJ   mother of the bride

A range of examples of alternate wording that can be used on wedding invitations:

THE BRIDE'S
MOTHER IS THE
ONLY HOSTESS

Mrs Christopher Wren
requests the pleasure of
your company at the marriage of her daughter

Jennifer

THE BRIDE'S
FATHER IS THE
ONLY HOST

Mr Christopher Wren
requests the pleasure of
your company at the marriage of his daughter

Jennifer

THE BRIDE'S
MOTHER AND
STEPFATHER ARE
THE HOST AND
HOSTESS

Mr and Mrs David Falconer
request the pleasure of
your company at the marriage of her daughter

Jennifer Wren

Note: The bride's surname may be included if she has not adopted her stepfather's name

THE BRIDE'S
FATHER AND
STEPMOTHER ARE
THE HOST AND
HOSTESS

Mr and Mrs Christopher Wren
request the pleasure of
your company at the marriage of his daughter

Jennifer

THE BRIDE'S
STEPMOTHER IS
THE HOSTESS

Mrs Christopher Wren
requests the pleasure of
your company at the marriage of her stepdaughter

Jennifer

THE BRIDE'S
PARENTS HAVE
DIVORCED BUT
THEY ARE THE
JOINT HOST AND
HOSTESS

Mr Christopher Wren and Mrs David Falconer *
request the pleasure of
your company at the marriage of their daughter

Jennifer

* '*Mrs Jane Wren*' *if she has not remarried*

41

THE BRIDE'S RELATIVES, GUARDIANS OR GODPARENTS ARE THE HOST AND HOSTESS

Admiral Sir John and Lady Fortescue
request the pleasure of
your company at the marriage of their niece/ward/goddaughter

Jennifer Wren

Note: The bride's surname may be included if it is different to that of the host and hostess

THE BRIDE IS THE HOSTESS

Miss Jennifer Wren
requests the pleasure of
your company at her marriage
to
Mr Robin Bird

THE BRIDE AND GROOM ARE THE HOST AND HOSTESS

Mr Robin Bird and Miss Jennifer Wren
request the pleasure of
your company at their marriage

Mr and Mrs Christopher Wren
request the pleasure of
your company at the reception following
the marriage of their daughter

Jennifer

Miss Jennifer Wren
requests the pleasure of
your company at the reception following
her marriage
to
Mr Robin Bird

Use the examples above, where applicable. If the bride is a widow, she is described as, for instance: 'Fleur, widow of Mr Michael Mont'.

If the bride's marriage has been dissolved, she is described as 'Mrs Fleur Mont'. If she has reverted to her maiden name, only her forename is necessary.

If the bride is the hostess, then follow the example above, with her name as 'Mrs Michael Mont' or 'Mrs Fleur Mont', as applicable.

Replying to Wedding Invitations

Replies should always be handwritten in the style below and sent on headed writing paper.
They are addressed to the hostess, even if it is a joint invitation from the host and hostess.

Reply in the third person

The date and time
must be reiterated

The date is written at
the bottom of the reply

Postponements and Cancellations

A card is usually sent out to announce the postponement or cancellation of a wedding.

This is generally $5^1/_2$ x $3^1/_2$ inches (14 x 9 cm), printed on white or cream card.

INDEFINITE POSTPONEMENT

If the wedding is indefinitely postponed invitations are sent out again when the new date has been fixed.

Similarly, if the wedding is to take place quietly, the second invitations are sent out by letter to near relations and close friends only.

Note that, barring the breaking off of the engagement, it is the invitations that are postponed or cancelled, not the wedding:

'Owing to the recent death of Colonel Samuel Braithwaite, Mr and Mrs John Blackwell deeply regret that they are obliged to cancel the invitations to the marriage of their daughter Elizabeth to Mr Mark Braithwaite on…'

POSTPONEMENT TO A LATER DATE

Example wording:

'Owing to the illness of Mrs Victor Scott, Mr and Mrs John Blank deeply regret that they are obliged to postpone the invitations to the marriage of their daughter Anne to Mr John Scott at St Margaret's Church, Westminster, from Tuesday, 12 December 2006 to Monday, 5 February 2007'

CANCELLATION BECAUSE THE WEDDING IS TO TAKE PLACE QUIETLY

Example wording:

'Owing to the recent death of her husband, Mrs John Black much regrets that she is obliged to cancel the invitations to the marriage of her daughter Lucinda to Captain Jonathan Trelawny, which will now take place very quietly on Tuesday 16 October 2007'

CANCELLATION BECAUSE THE ENGAGEMENT IS BROKEN OFF

Example wording:

'Sir John and Lady Hopley announce that the marriage of their daughter Sophie to Mr Christopher Camberley, which was arranged for Tuesday 17 July 2007, will now not take place'

Social
Events

Table Plans

General Points and Royal Guests

There are clear guidelines but these have been modified by the relaxation of the rules of precedence.

It remains essential to accord pre-eminence to senior members of the Royal Family and to respect tradition where their retinues are concerned but, other than this, common sense should be employed. Whereas in some situations social rank may still be deemed to be of the utmost importance, at the majority of functions considerations such as professional status and age are now treated as equally or more powerfully determining factors.

The nature of the occasion provides the most telling guide and should offer indications as to the relative significance of guests. Clearly, a guest of honour must be seated so as to reflect his or her status and, by way of example, the chairman of a host company, the MP of the constituency in which a function is held, a foreign dignitary whose country is being honoured, or a benefactor should all be recognised and seated appropriately.

ROYAL PROGRESS

When the Sovereign attends a function, the host surrenders his place and takes up the place on the Sovereign's right.

Other members of the Royal Family entitled to the prefix Royal Highness are given special precedence.

SPOUSES OF ROYAL GUESTS

The husband of a female member of the Royal Family is accorded precedence immediately after her when both attend a function. If he attends alone he retains his own precedence unless he is the principal guest.

RETINUES

The suite in attendance on a member of the Royal Family should be placed reasonably near to the royal guest.

TABLE PLAN APPROVAL

The top table plan of any function attended by the Sovereign or any other member of the Royal Family must be submitted for prior approval to the Private Secretary, from whom the names of the suite in attendance should also be obtained.

No guest should leave a function before a member of the Royal Family, except in special circumstances, when prior permission should be obtained.

LEAVING FUNCTIONS   This rule may be honoured in the breach rather than in the observance at charity balls and other functions which continue after midnight. Equally, the organiser of an evening function may seek, through the Private Secretary, blanket permission for guests to leave before the member of the Royal Family.

A guest who is required to leave a function at an appointed hour, before the member of the Royal Family, should seek permission to do so, through the Private Secretary, in advance of the function.

SPECIMEN TABLE PLAN   The table plan below is for a civic function at which the Lord and Lady Mayoress of a city are host and hostess, using only one side of the top table, and with husbands and wives seated together.

Seating plan

Centre of table	Bishop
	Bishop's wife
	Swiss Ambassador
	High Sheriff's wife
	High Sheriff
	Lady Mayoress (hostess)
	Lord Mayor (host)
	The Queen
	Lord-Lieutenant
	Lord-Lieutenant's wife
	Chairman of the County Council
	Chairman of the County Council's wife
	Marquess of Portsdown
	Marchioness of Portsdown
	Home Secretary
	Home Secretary's wife

Principal guests:

HM The Queen

The Lord-Lieutenant of the county and his wife

The High Sheriff of the county and his wife

The chairman of the County Council and his wife

The Swiss Ambassador (male, not married)

The Marquess and Marchioness of Portsdown

The Anglican Bishop of the Diocese and his wife

The Home Secretary and his wife

Official Functions

The principal guest is placed on the host's right. Traditionally, the principal guest's wife would be placed on the host's left, the host's wife being placed on the right of the principal guest.

If wives are not present, the second most important guest would be placed on the host's left.

It is now almost as likely for the host, or the principal guest, to be a woman, in which case the same basic principles may be applied to their logical conclusion and juggling employed to achieve the desired balance.

REPRESENTATION When the principal guest is the Sovereign or other head of state, a member of the Royal Family, a Prime Minister, a member of the Cabinet or someone of comparable importance, the need to invite some or all of the following, and their partners, should be considered:

> The Lord-Lieutenant of the county
> The Lord Mayor, Lord Provost, Mayor or Provost of the city, borough etc.
> The High Sheriff of the county
> The chairman of the county council

Those who accept would be placed in this order of precedence after such principal guests.

LORD MAYORS The Lord Mayor of London has precedence throughout his City immediately after the Sovereign and elsewhere immediately after earls.

Other Lord Mayors and Mayors (Provosts and Lord Provosts in Scotland), as well as council chairmen, have precedence immediately after the Royal Family on their own civic premises and after the Lord-Lieutenant elsewhere in their city or borough.

On relevant occasions these guests may, as a courtesy, yield their prime places to a guest of honour, or, for example, to an archbishop at a church function.

Outside their areas of jurisdiction all except the Lord Mayor of London have no precedence other than that which courtesy, or the occasion, may demand.

DIPLOMATS Ambassadors, high commissioners and chargés d'affaires should be placed at the top table, their relative precedence being strictly observed.

As a general rule, diplomatic representatives from countries that do not enjoy diplomatic relations with each other should not be invited to the same function. When, as sometimes happens, it is necessary to invite them, care should be taken to avoid placing them near to each other.

MINISTERS AND PRIVY COUNSELLORS   Ministers of the Crown and Privy Counsellors should be placed at the top table.

THE CHURCH   Important dignitaries of the established church are placed high among the guests. High dignitaries of other churches should, as a courtesy, be accorded status immediately succeeding those of the same rank from the established church.

OTHER PLACEMENTS   When a function takes place within premises belonging to some organisation other than the host's a senior representative of that organisation should be invited and placed high among the guests.

Other important guests are placed in order of precedence and importance, subject to the following general rules:

Important members of the governing body should be interspersed among the principal guests.

Guests' partners should be placed according to the precedence of the guest invited in their own right.

It is up to the host to decide whether husbands and wives are to be seated together or apart.

The former is easier to arrange; the latter, which is always followed at private functions, gives both husband and wife a chance to meet new people.

A function given by a society at which the president is the host, accompanied by his wife, using both side of the top table.

Principal guests:

Their Royal Highnesses the Duke and Duchess of Kent
The Lord-Lieutenant of the county and his wife
The Mayor and Mayoress of the borough
The Vice-Chancellor of the local university and his wife
The Naval Flag Officer of the area and his wife
A Roman Catholic Bishop

		R.C. Bishop
		Vice-Chanellor's wife
Wife of Naval Flag Officer		Mayor
Lord-Lieutenant		Duchess of Kent
Wife of President *(Hostess)*	Centre of table	President of the Society *(Host)*
Duke of Kent		Lord-Lieutenant's wife
Mayoress		Naval Flag Officer
Vice-Chancellor		

Private Functions

The host is customarily seated at one end of the table, the hostess at the other. Alternatively, the host may be seated in the centre of one side of the table and the hostess immediately opposite him.

PLACEMENT The principal male guest is placed on the right of the hostess and his wife on the right of the host. The other seating is largely a matter for the hostess to decide according to the mutual interests of the guests.

Exceptionally, if the party numbers eight, the hostess may give up her place to the chief male guest: otherwise it is impracticable to preserve the rule of seating the sexes alternately. If a party numbers six or ten (that is, in multiples of four in addition to the host and hostess), the table is easier to arrange by placing men and women alternately, but today this custom is not too rigidly applied.

COUPLES In general, couples are not seated together, with the exception of those engaged to be married or in their first year of marriage.

PRECEDENCE Strict order of precedence need not be observed, but should not be ignored. Indeed, care should still be taken to ensure that the diplomatic precedence of high commissioners and ambassadors is observed.

MR JOHN NEWLYWED	MRS SUSAN NEWLYWED	MRS ANTHONY BROWN	MAYOR

HOST ... HOSTESS

MAYOR'S WIFE	THE REVEREND JOHN JONES	MRS ROBERT GREEN (a widow)	MR ANTHONY BROWN

Guest Lists

Guests may be shown where they are placed at table in various ways. For a party not exceeding 30, a seating plan may be displayed. For a party of up to 100, a numbered drawing of the table may be displayed with a list of guests alongside it in alphabetical order, each with a seat number.

For parties of more than 100, each guest should be provided with a printed table plan, with the names listed in alphabetical order, or with a table diagram with their seat marked. Male guests without title or rank should be styled Mr. When both husbands and wives are invited, the solecism of mixing styles – for example, John Brown, Esq and Mrs John Brown – must be avoided.

STYLES BY OFFICE	Any guest invited by virtue of office should be so indicated: for example, Fenchurch, Sir William, KBE, President of the Society of Stationers.
PEERS	Peers are shown by their exact rank in the peerage. For example, Middlesex, The Earl of, KBE; Flintshire, The Countess of. The word 'The' is optional for viscounts, barons, their wives and widows. They must all be styled in the same way within the list, except for peers by courtesy, who do not have the prefix 'The'.

The prefix appropriate to the grade of peer may be shown if desired:

  (i)   His or Her Grace for a duke or duchess
  (ii)   The Most Hon for a marquess or marchioness
  (iii)   The Right Hon for other peers and peeresses (if this prefix is used, all peers and peeresses, apart from those by courtesy, should be treated similarly)

PEERS BY COURTESY	Peers and peeresses by courtesy, and former wives of peers, have no peerage prefix (neither The Right Hon etc. nor The). The courtesy style of The Hon is shown.
PRIVY COUNSELLORS	Privy counsellors are given the prefix The Right Hon but not the suffix PC, except for those who are also members of the peerage.
BARONETS	Baronets are shown with the suffix of Bt.
HONOURS AND DECORATIONS	Honours and decorations, and degrees when appropriate, should be included, as well as other principal awards, such as fellowships of learned societies.

Place Cards

Place cards should be always be handwritten, and the names kept brief, with honours, decorations, degrees etc. omitted.

PEERS	The formal prefix for peers should also be omitted.
	They are shown as, for example, The Earl of Blank or Lord Whyte.
PRIVY COUNSELLORS	The Right Hon is retained for privy counsellors who are not peers.
SUFFIXES	The suffixes Bt, RN, QC and MP are also retained for those so entitled.
STYLES BY OFFICE	Any office held should be omitted, except that important guests should be indicated by their office instead of their name.
	For example, The Swiss Ambassador, The Lord Mayor.
THE HONOURABLE	The Hon is usually shown before the name at a public function but omitted at a private party.
UNTITLED GENTLEMEN	Mr invariably takes the place of Esq.

Toasts & Speeches

Toasts

Grace is usually said before a meal and sometimes afterwards, in which case it precedes the loyal toast(s). There is no preamble to grace. The toastmaster announces only: 'Pray silence for grace by your President', or 'by Canon John Jones' etc. The member of clergy's living should not be mentioned: that is, not 'The Rt Rev John Jones, Bishop of Wrexham'.

A bishop may be asked to say grace; if his chaplain is present, it is customary for the latter to do so.

LOYAL TOAST The first and principal loyal toast, as approved by the Queen, is 'The Queen'.

It is incorrect to use such forms as 'I give you the loyal toast of Her Majesty The Queen'.

To obtain the necessary silence, the toastmaster may say, without preamble, 'Pray silence for…'.

SECOND LOYAL TOAST The second loyal toast which, if given, immediately follows the first, is likewise limited to: 'The Prince Philip, Duke of Edinburgh, The Prince of Wales and the other members of the Royal Family'.

SMOKING Guests do not smoke until after the loyal toast(s). The announcement 'Ladies and Gentlemen, you may now smoke' is superfluous unless the Queen is present, when it is necessary to announce: 'Ladies and Gentlemen, you have Her Majesty's permission to smoke'.

COUNTY OF LANCASTER The loyal toast in Lancashire, Greater Manchester and Merseyside follows the traditional wording used in the old County of Lancaster: that is, 'The Queen, Duke of Lancaster'. This toast is used throughout the northwest of England and at Lancastrian organisations elsewhere.

JERSEY In Jersey the toast of 'The Queen, our Duke' (Duke of Normandy) is local and unofficial, and used when only islanders are present. This toast is not used in the other Channel Islands.

Speeches

It is impossible to give a list of those who should be mentioned in the preamble of a speech, since this depends so much on those present at a particular function. In general, however, the list should be kept as short as possible, avoiding any omission which would cause justifiable offence. The speaker does not, of course, include himself in this preamble.

HM THE QUEEN   Should the Queen be present, a preamble begins 'May it please Your Majesty'.

THE HOST   With the above exception, a preamble begins with the host, who is referred to by office. For example:

> Madam President
> Mr Chairman
> Provost

PRESIDENT   If a president is also a member of the Royal Family, they should be referred to as 'Your Royal Highness and President'.

A non-royal duke or duchess is addressed as 'Your Grace and President'.

A peer other than a duke is addressed as 'My Lord and President'. It is incorrect to use the form 'My Lord President', except for the Lord President of the Council.

A woman, either titled or untitled, with the exception of a member of the Royal Family or a duchess, is referred to as 'Madam President'. An untitled man is referred to as 'Mr President'.

VICE-PRESIDENT   When a vice-president takes the chair, he or she may be referred to as 'Mr Vice-President' or 'Madam Vice-President' as appropriate, with the relevant prefix mentioned above, but he or she is more usually referred to as 'Mr Chairman' or 'Madam Chairman'.

CHAIRMAN   A chairman is called 'Mr Chairman' or 'Madam Chairman', irrespective of his or her rank, with the exception of a member of the Royal Family, who is referred to as 'Your Royal Highness'. A peer should not be called 'My Lord Chairman'.

If a vice-chairman, managing director or other officer of the organisation takes the chair, he or she is still referred to as 'Mr Chairman' or 'Madam Chairman'. The use of these expressions is not restricted to the actual chairman of the organisation.

The following list gives the form in which other important guests should be included in a preamble in order of precedence, after those previously mentioned:

> Your Royal Highness
> My Lord Mayor (My Lord Provost etc.) *See (i)*
> Mr Recorder (outside London)
> Mr Chairman of the…County Council (outside Greater London)
> My Lord Chancellor
> Prime Minister (or, more formally, Mr Prime Minister) *See (ii)*
> Your Excellency(ies) *See (iii)*
> Your Grace(s) *See (iv)*
> My Lord(s) *See (v)*
> Ladies and Gentlemen *See (vi)*

(i)   This applies only to the civic head of the city, borough etc. in which the function takes place. A civic head from elsewhere is mentioned after 'My Lord(s)'. More than one Lord Mayor or Lord Provost may be covered by 'My Lord Mayors', 'My Lord Provosts' or by naming each. There is no plural for Mr Mayor; 'Your Worships' is used.

(ii)   Also:
My Lord President (that is, of the Privy Council)
My Lord Privy Seal
Mr Chancellor (of the Exchequer or of the Duchy of Lancaster)
Minister(s) (this covers a secretary of state. Other ministers are not mentioned in a preamble when the Prime Minister attends a function)

(iii)   Ambassadors and high commissioners

(iv)   This covers dukes and duchesses. If the Archbishop of Canterbury is present, 'Your Grace' (or 'Your Graces' if a duke or duchess is also attending) should be mentioned before 'My Lord Chancellor'. Similarly, the Archbishop of York is covered by including 'Your Grace' immediately after 'My Lord Chancellor'. Both archbishops rank before ambassadors and high commissioners.

(v)   For peers other than dukes, peers by courtesy, for diocesan bishops by right and for other bishops by courtesy. In the absence of any peers, the form 'My Lord Bishops' may be used.

(vi)   When only one woman is present the form should be 'Lady (or 'My Lady' if titled) and Gentlemen' or 'Mrs/Lady Blank, Gentlemen'; never 'Madam and Gentlemen'.

ROMAN CATHOLIC DIGNITARIES	A cardinal archbishop may be included in the form 'Your Eminence', placed by courtesy after 'Your Grace(s)'.
	Other archbishops and bishops are by courtesy mentioned in the same way as those of the Anglican Communion.
OTHER CLERGY	Clergy, other than archbishops and bishops, should not be included. In particular, the forms 'Reverend Sir' and 'Reverend Father' are archaic. Exceptionally, 'Mr Dean', 'Mr Provost' or 'Archdeacon' may be included.
GUEST OF HONOUR	When the guest of honour is not covered by one of the above terms, he or she is included in the preamble by office immediately before 'Ladies and Gentlemen'.
	This specific mention also applies when an individual who is present has provided the building in which the function is taking place.
ALDERMEN AND SHERIFFS	Within the City of London it is customary to refer to these as 'Mr Alderman' or 'Aldermen' and 'Mr Sheriff' or 'Sheriffs' immediately before 'Ladies and Gentlemen'.
	Elsewhere, 'Councillors' may be included at civic functions immediately before 'Ladies and Gentlemen'.
THE ENDING	A speaker proposing a toast should make this clear at the end of the speech in some such form as: 'I give you the toast of…' or 'I ask you to rise and drink to the toast of…'. This obviates any need for the toastmaster to say, 'The toast is…'.
TOASTMASTER	The toastmaster should be given the form in which he is to make all announcements in writing.
SPEAKERS	A speaker is announced by name, followed by office where applicable. For example, '…the Right Honourable John Jones, Her Majesty's Secretary of State for …'.
FIRST SPEAKER	For the first speaker the announcement should have a preamble, as for the speech, followed by, 'Pray silence for…'.
SUBSEQUENT SPEAKERS	For subsequent announcements the preamble should be omitted.

Visiting Cards

Visiting cards are now seldom seen, but their usage does persist in some areas as a pleasing social convention. They are traditionally engraved from a copperplate, but printing is a suitable alternative.

GENTLEMEN'S CARDS A gentleman's card is usually 3 x 1¹/₂ inches (7.6 x 3.8 cm). It should give no more than a title, rank, private or Service address (two if desired) and club.

LADIES' CARDS A lady's card is traditionally larger than a gentleman's, usually 3¹/₄ x 2¹/₄ inches (8.3 x 5.7 cm), though 3¹/₂ x 2¹/₂ inches (8.9 x 6.4 cm) is sometimes used. Some women prefer a smaller card of the same size as a gentleman's.

Joint cards, or those for families, should be the same size as a lady's card.

TITLES The name of a peer or peeress is shown by his or her grade, but with no prefix, not even 'The'. For example, Duke of Norfolk, Earl of Lonsdale.

Courtesy styles derived from a peerage are shown in such form as Lord John Jones, Lady Emily Jones etc., but Honourable is not used: those so styled are shown as Mr, Mrs, Ms or Miss as applicable.

BARONETS AND KNIGHTS A baronet or knight is shown as Sir John Jones, that is without the suffix Bt or Bart, and his wife as Lady Jones.

OTHER STYLES The only other prefixes used on cards are ecclesiastical titles, ranks in the Armed Forces and doctor or professor. Untitled men precede their name with Mr, followed by their forename and initials, except that the head of a family may traditionally style himself Mr Forsyte, i.e. without forename or initials.

A married woman may use her husband's forename or initials, although this rule is no longer an absolute. The senior married woman in a family (i.e. the wife of the eldest surviving son) may style herself Mrs Forsyte, without forename or initials. A widow traditionally uses the same style as during her husband's lifetime. A divorced woman always uses her own forename or initials.

Suffixes are never used on visiting cards, except those that indicate membership of the Armed Forces.

An archbishop, bishop, dean or archdeacon shows his territorial appointment: for example, The Archbishop of Canterbury, The Bishop of Wakefield, The Dean of Norwich or The Archdeacon of Lincoln.

ECCLESIASTICAL RANK

A canon or prebendary is usually so styled without appending 'The Reverend', such as Canon John Jones or Prebendary J W H Jones.

A retired bishop is styled by his prefix. That is, The Right Reverend John Jones. The style Bishop Jones is not normally used.

An archdeacon emeritus is styled Archdeacon Jones, with the personal choice of adding forenames or initials. Alternatively, the prefix 'The Venerable' may be used, in which case the use of forenames or initials is obligatory.

Other members of the clergy are styled The Reverend Jane Jones or The Reverend J W Jones. Reverend may be abbreviated to Rev or Revd.

ARMED FORCES

Officers in the Armed Forces use their rank in full: abbreviations such as Lt-Col should be avoided.

Exceptions are naval officers below the rank of lieutenant, Army and Royal Marines officers below the rank of captain and Royal Air Force officers below the rank of flight lieutenant, all of whom are styled Mr, Mrs, Ms or Miss as applicable.

A naval officer below the rank of rear admiral places Royal Navy or Royal Naval Reserve below and slightly to the right of the name.

An Army or Royal Marines officer on the active list below the rank of colonel places his regiment or corps, or its accepted abbreviation, below his name.

A Royal Air Force officer below the rank of air commodore places Royal Air Force, which may be abbreviated to RAF, below and slightly to the right of his name.

Retired officers do not include Retired or Retd, with the exception of the Royal Navy, where Retd is occasionally added below and slightly to the right of the name if there is a special reason for doing so.

A retired army or Royal Marines officer omits his former regiment or corps.

Lists of Names

Names on programmes, brochures etc. were traditionally listed in order of precedence. However, this practice is falling into disuse as it is both complicated and old-fashioned.

An acceptable solution is to list names in alphabetical order, the sole exception being that the Sovereign and other members of the Royal Family must come first.

Members of the Royal Family are always shown with the royal style, usually in full: that is, 'Her Royal Highness…'

Others should be treated consistently, either in the formal or social style, whichever is to be adopted.

FORMAL STYLE

His Grace the Duke of Blank
Her Grace the Duchess of Blank
Her Grace Mary, Duchess of Blank
The Rt Hon the Earl of Blank
The Rt Hon the Lord Blank
His Grace the Archbishop of Blank
  or The Most Reverend the Lord Archbishop of Blank
The Rt Rev the Lord Bishop of Blank
The Very Rev the Dean of Blank
The Rev John Smith
The Rt Hon John Brown

SOCIAL STYLE

The Duke of Blank
The Duchess of Blank
Mary, Duchess of Blank
The Earl of Blank
The Lord Blank
The Lord Archbishop of Blank
The Lord Bishop of Blank
The Dean of Blank
The Rev John Smith
The Rt Hon John Brown

PEERS

There is no rule for the position of 'the' in lists of peers: for example, Rt Hon the Earl of Blank, The Rt Hon Viscount Blank or Rt Hon Lord Blank are not incorrect, but the usage listed is recommended.

Similarly, it is not laid down whether one should use upper or lower case for the first letter of 'the' within a sentence, except that the former must always be accorded to the Queen in formal address.

Peers and peeresses are given the territorial designation only if it forms an integral part of the title; for example, Viscount Montgomery of Alamein.

Peers and peeresses by courtesy and former wives of peers are not accorded 'the' or any formal prefix.

UNTITLED MEN

Untitled men are either consistently shown as John Smith, Esq or as Mr John Smith and doctors (holders of academic degrees) as John Smith, Esq, DSc or Dr John Smith (not Dr John Smith, DSc).

OFFICIAL LISTS

As a general rule, the form used on an official or similar list should be as for addressing an envelope, except that if the list is in alphabetical order, the name should come first. For example:

Baxter, Admiral Sir George, KCB, DSO
Baxter, Lady
Beecher, Edward J, MP
Beecher, Mrs Edward
Bilston, The Very Reverend John, KCVO, DD
Bilston, Mrs John
Bosham, The Right Hon the Earl of, PC
Bosham, The Right Hon the Countess of
Brook, The Right Hon Richard, MP
Bullion, Colonel P R, MC, JP, DL
Bullion, Mrs P R
Burton, The Worshipful the Mayor of

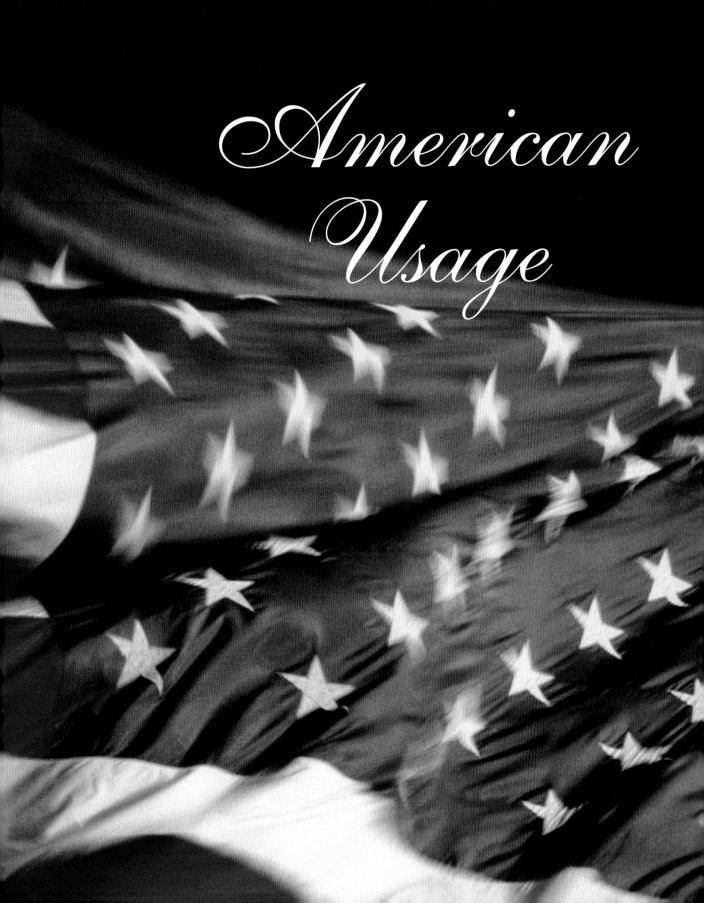

American
Usage

Titles & Styles

HONORABLE

Honorable is used officially by the following, when they are addressed by name:

American ambassadors
American ministers (with governmental powers)
American representatives on international organisations
Deputy and assistant heads of independent government agencies
Assistant secretaries of executive departments and officers of comparable rank
Assistants and special assistants to the President
Cabinet officers
Clerk of the United States House of Representatives
Commissioners
The Commissioner of the District of Columbia
Counsellor of the Department of State
Foreign ministers
Governors of states and territories
Heads of major organisations within the Federal Agencies
Heads of international organisations, alternates, deputies and assistant heads
High officers of state governments
Judges (except justices of the Supreme Court)
Legal adviser and officers of comparable rank
Mayors of cities
Ministers resident
President of the United States
Public printer
Congressmen and women
Secretary of the United States Senate
Senators
Sergeant at Arms of the United States Senate and House of Representatives
State senators
State cabinet and legislative officials
Under-secretaries and officers of comparable rank of executive departments
United States representatives, alternates and deputies of international
    organisations and organs of such organisations
Vice-President

'The Honorable' appears on the first line of the envelope, above the forename and surname on the second line, and a little to the left. It is not used when issuing or answering invitations.

The word 'Honorable' is not used in conjunction with the prefix of Mr, Mrs, Miss, Ms, Dr, a rank in the Services or an academic degree (i.e. the style remains The Honorable John Smith). Informally, it may be abbreviated to The Hon or Hon.

The title is not usually used as a term of direct address, but is added when making formal introductions, followed by the first name and surname.

Its use is normally continued for life by those in more senior positions, but not usually by those who have held state or regional appointments.

HIS OR HER EXCELLENCY

The title of His Excellency is not officially used by the Department of State, but is the usual form of address for Roman Catholic archbishops and bishops.

It is often the social form for state governors and American ambassadors. Foreign presidents, ambassadors and others bear the style officially and socially.

The usual practice is to write His/Her Excellency in full on the line above the name and a little to the left. More informally, it is abbreviated to HE before the name.

His/Her Excellency is not used when issuing or answering invitations.

CONVERSATION WITH OFFICIALS

No surnames are used when one speaks to an official, only the title. This is not the case when one addresses an associate justice of the Supreme Court as several people hold this position. It is correct to address all of these, once engaged in conversation, as Sir or Madam.

THE PRESIDENT AND FIRST LADY

The President is addressed as Mr President. In conversation he may subsequently be called Sir.

The First Lady is addressed, verbally and in writing, as any other married woman. e.g. Mrs Washington. The couple are addressed as The President and Mrs Washington.

Thank you letters for functions at the White House are written to the First Lady.

SENATORS

When several members of the Senate are present at the same function, the Senator who has served the longest period in the United States Senate takes precedence.

A Senator does not use this appointment on invitations or visiting cards, but the name of the state represented is engraved in the lower right hand side of the card.

ARMED FORCES

The Air Force and the Marine Corps have identical commissioned ranks as the Army. All ranks are preferably written out in full on the envelope.

After the name it is permissible to abbreviate the service:

United States Navy	USN
United States Army	USA
United States Air Force	USAF
United States Marine Corps	USMC
United States Army Reserve	USAR
United States Naval Reserve	USNR
United States Coast Guard	USCG
Army of the United States	AUS
United States Marine Corps Reserve	USMCR

It is incorrect to write to officers by their rank without their name, such as 'Dear Colonel'. Verbally, a general, lieutenant general, major general and brigadier general are all called General.

Similarly, an admiral, vice admiral and rear admiral are called Admiral. This is the same as the British practice. They are addressed socially as, for example, General Robert Brown or Admiral Charles Hoffmann, and this is the invariable practice in a joint communication with their wives.

MR AND ESQ

Mr is the generally accepted prefix in the United States.

Esquire, usually abbreviated to Esq, is customarily used in social correspondence, especially in the eastern part of the United States.

In business circles, Esquire is used for lawyers and Justices of the Peace. In the Department of State, the term is reserved for Foreign Service officers serving abroad and is not abbreviated.

DOCTOR OF MEDICINE

Although referred to as Doctor verbally and at the beginning of a letter, a doctor of medicine is addressed on the envelope as 'John K Smith, MD'.

NUMERALS, SENIOR AND JUNIOR

The practice of using numerals, Senior or Junior after names is widespread. When a father – who was not previously known as Junior (Jr) or by a numeral – has a son who is given the same forename, the son is called Jr.

The father may then use Senior (Sr) after his name, but some consider that the best American usage does not use Sr. The father would continue to be known as Mr John Howard. His widow might subsequently add Sr to her name to distinguish herself from her daughter-in-law, or the son and daughter-in-law may retain the Jr status in respect to the widow.

If the son, Jr, has a son with the same name born during his grandfather's lifetime, then the child would have the numeral III. Hereafter the usage is optional, but a few families maintain their numerals for several generations with impressive results.

Traditionally, the use of II is not adopted by the Sr's son (Jr). It refers to another relative of the same forename and surname, often a grandson or nephew, who is not necessarily in direct succession. This is no longer a common practice.

Styles by Office

	SALUTATION	ENVELOPE	VERBAL ADDRESS	CONVERSATION
President	Dear Mr (Madam) President	The President	Mr President	Mr President, subsequently Sir
Vice-President	Dear Mr (Madam) Vice-President	The Vice-President	Mr Vice-President	Mr Vice-President
Speaker of the House of Representatives	Dear Mr (Madam) Speaker	The Honorable (full name) The Speaker of the House of Representatives	Mr Speaker, or by name	Mr Speaker, or by name

	SALUTATION	ENVELOPE	VERBAL ADDRESS	CONVERSATION
Chief Justice	My dear Mr Chief Justice	The Chief Justice	Mr Chief Justice, or by name	Mr Chief Justice, or by name
Ambassador of the United States	My dear Madam Ambassador	The Honorable (full name) The American Ambassador	Madam Ambassador, or by name	Madam Ambassador, or by name
Foreign Ambassadors in Washington	Your Excellency	The Excellency (full name) The Ambassador of (country)	Your Excellency or Mr Ambassador or by name	Mr Ambassador or name
Associate Justice of the Supreme Court	Dear Mr (Madam) Justice Frankfurter	Mr Justice Frankfurter	Mr Justice Frankfurter	Mr Justice Frankfurter
Members of the Cabinet	Dear Mr (Madam) Secretary	The Honorable (full name) The Secretary of State	Mr Secretary	The Secretary of State
Senator	My dear Senator Doolittle	The Honorable Tom Doolittle United States Senate	Senator or Senator Doolittle	Senator Doolittle
Governor of State	My dear Governor Bronson	The Honorable Chad Bronson Governor of Georgia	Govenor or Governor Bronson	The Governor of Georgia
Member of the House of Representatives	Dear Mr (Miss/Mrs/Ms) Washington	The Honorable Bette Washington United States House of Representatives	Miss Washington	Miss Washington
Retired President	Dear Mr Doolittle	The Honorable Tom Doolittle	Mr Doolittle	Former President Doolittle (formal), Mr Doolittle (social)

Members of the Cabinet are addressed as Mr (or Madam) Secretary, but the Attorney General is addressed as 'Mr Attorney General'. A governor of a state is officially designated The Honorable.

The valediction for the President/Vice-President is 'Respectfully Yours' or 'Sincerely'. For all others, use 'Sincerely' or 'Sincerely Yours'.

Visiting Cards

RESIDENCE

Visiting cards are used to announce that a call has been made and to provide contact details. They may be engraved or printed; thick paper stock must be used.

The residential address should appear in the lower right hand corner, but is not always included. The card may only give a telephone number and email address.

BUSINESS USE

A business card may be used for social purposes. This is only acceptable if a personal card is not available. The card should be amended with details such as home telephone number or email address.

Conversely, a personal card may be used for business.

Invitations

Formal Invitations

Formal invitations should be a minimum of $4 \times 5\frac{1}{2}$ inches (10 x 14 cm), and are placed unfolded in an envelope. The name of the guest is handwritten on a formal invitation, but the rest of the card is engraved or printed.

If the invitation is to a very large function, such as one given by the president of a society, the guest's name is omitted. The wording reads 'request the pleasure of your company at a reception in honour of…'. 'Honour' is spelt in the English way.

For very large functions, engraved or printed reply cards are enclosed in the envelope with the invitation.

Formal engraved reminder cards are occasionally sent when no answer has been received by the hostess.

FORMAL REPLIES   A formal reply should be handwritten and would read:

Mr and Mrs David Falconer

accept with pleasure

the kind invitation

of Charlotte and Christopher Wren

to a supper dance in honour of Jennifer and Robert

Friday, January fourteenth

at nine o'clock in the evening

The Rainbow Room

30 Rockefeller Plaza

Informal Invitations

Informal invitations are often given verbally, or sent via email. If a written invitation is sent, this may be a printed card, personalised visiting card or fill-in invitation.

STANDARD INVITATION CARDS   For regular hosts, it is usual to use standard invitation cards. Generally these give the host's name and address, and a request for attendance.

They are printed or engraved with designated spaces for details of the particular function.

SPECIAL GUESTS   If invited to meet a special guest, the line 'in honour of…' may be added after the type of function. Note that 'honour' is spelt in the English way.

INFORMAL DANCES   Guests' names may be omitted on an invitation to an informal dance, when the wording is 'request the pleasure of your company at a small dance', etc.

REPLIES   An informal invitation is answered in the manner in which it is received, i.e. by email, verbally or a short handwritten note to the host or hostess.

Informal drinks' party

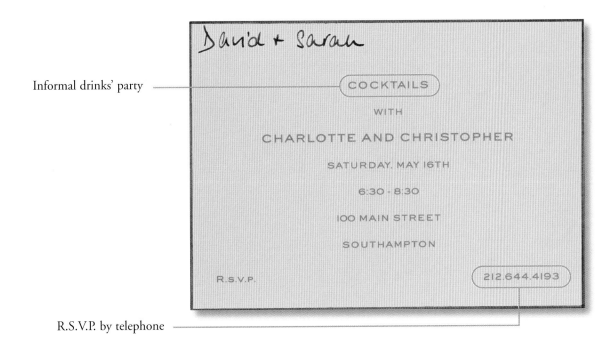

David + Sarah

COCKTAILS

WITH

CHARLOTTE AND CHRISTOPHER

SATURDAY, MAY 16TH

6:30 - 8:30

100 MAIN STREET

SOUTHAMPTON

R.S.V.P.   212.644.4193

R.S.V.P. by telephone

Charlotte + Christopher

You are cordially invited to a brunch for

Jennifer & Robin

on Sunday, the twenty-second of April
at one o'clock

Swifty's
1007 Lexington Avenue
New York

R.s.v.p.
212.644.4193

The date is usually
written out in full

Wedding Invitations

ENVELOPES

Invitations should be sent out in two envelopes. The outer envelope is addressed with the full name of the guests, i.e. 'Mr and Mrs David Falconer'. The inner envelope is addressed to 'Mr and Mrs Falconer', left unsealed, facing the back of the outside envelope. It is usual to leave the tissue paper on the invitation.

The envelope for formal ceremonies is addressed to both husband and wife, but each child in the family must receive a separate invitation.

WORDING

The phrase 'honour of your presence' is used for a religious ceremony ('honour' spelt in the English way). 'The pleasure of your company' is used for a wedding reception. For informal weddings or commitment ceremonies, phrases such as 'invite you to share' or 'join us in celebrating' are often used.

TYPES OF INVITATION

Guests are often invited to the ceremony, but not to the reception or, conversely, only to the reception. Consequently, there are four combinations:

(i) A single invitation to both the church and the reception. This is also adopted if the wedding guests automatically continue to the reception.

(ii) When more guests are invited to the wedding than the reception, a smaller, engraved stiff card for the reception, measuring about 4 x 3 inches (10 x 8 cm), is sent out with the full size wedding invitation.

(iii) A large card to the reception only, with the words 'request the pleasure of your company' in place of 'the honour of your presence', and 'at the wedding reception of their daughter' in place of 'at the marriage of their daughter'.

(iv) When more guests are invited to the reception than the wedding, a large card, which is identical to the previous example, is used to invite guests to the reception and a smaller card (see above) is used to invite the guests to the church.

INVITATIONS TO A HOUSE CEREMONY

The address of the house takes the place of the church on invitations to a house wedding or commitment ceremony. If the wedding takes place at a house other than the hosts', the wording is 'at the house of Mr and Mrs Warren, Campville, Albany'. All guests are automatically invited to the reception.

Formal wedding and commitment ceremony invitations must be ——————— engraved, usually on thick cream paper

Mr & Mrs David Falconer

Mrs. Robert Johnson

Mr. Christopher Wren

request the honour of your presence

at the marriage of their daughter

Jennifer

to

Mr. Robert Bird

Saturday, the twentieth of May

at five o'clock

St. James Episcopal Church

Madison Avenue at Seventy-first Street

New York City

An engraved invitation to only the church does not require an answer; otherwise the wording of a reply follows the invitation ———————

Forms of Address

The Royal Family

The Queen

The very formal style of ending letters is still used in correspondence with the Queen. With the exception of personal friends, letters are sent via the private secretary, equerry or lady-in-waiting of the particular member of the Royal Family.

The letter should be addressed to the holder of the office and not by name, even if it is known, but subsequent correspondence should be sent to the writer of the reply.

COMMUNICATIONS FROM THOSE KNOWN PERSONALLY	For those who wish to communicate directly with the Queen, the following style is used:
	The letter should begin 'Madam' or 'May it please Your Majesty' and end 'I have the honour to remain, Madam, Your Majesty's most humble and obedient servant'. The word 'remain' can be replaced with 'be' if desired.
	In the body of the letter 'Your Majesty' should be substituted for 'you' and 'Your Majesty's' for 'your'
	The envelope should be addressed to 'Her Majesty The Queen'.
VERBAL ADDRESS	'Your Majesty' for the first time and subsequently 'Ma'am'. This should always rhyme with 'Pam'. Pronunciation to rhyme with 'palm' has not been correct for some generations.
DESCRIPTION IN CONVERSATION	'Her Majesty' or 'The Queen', as appropriate.
CONVERSATION	In conversation with the Queen 'Your Majesty' should be substituted for 'you'. References to other members of the Royal Family are made to 'His (or Her) Royal Highness' or the appropriate title, such as the Duke of Edinburgh or Princess Royal.
	When introducing another person to the Queen it is only necessary to state the name of the person to be introduced: 'May I present John Smith, Your Majesty?'

Sir David Carpenter Memorial Foundation
Blank House
Blankville
Blankshire
BL1 A23

15 August 2006

Letters are sent to the private secretary

Dear Sir,

I would be most grateful if you would ask Her Majesty The Queen if she would consider visiting the Sir David Carpenter Memorial Sculpture Park, Blankshire.

The park commemorates Sir David's life and work by displaying his sculptures together for the first time in the grounds of Blank House, Sir David's home for more than forty years.

Please could you submit, for Her Majesty's consideration, an invitation to visit the Park during June, prior to it's opening to the public at the beginning of July?

Sign off to reflect the salutation of 'Dear Sir'

Yours faithfully,

S Wren

Sarah Wren
Treasurer, Sir David Carpenter Memorial Foundation

Other members of the Royal Family

The rules of correspondence with other members of the Royal Family follow those for writing to the Queen. That is, unless the writer is personally known to the prince, princess, duke, etc., concerned, it is usual practice to write to the equerry, private secretary or lady-in-waiting.

Letters should be addressed to the holder of the office and not by name. Subsequent correspondence should be sent to the writer of the reply.

COMMUNICATIONS FROM THOSE KNOWN PERSONALLY

For those who wish to communicate directly with a member of the Royal Family the following style is used:

The letter should begin 'Sir/Madam' and end 'I have the honour to remain, Sir/Madam, Your Royal Highness's most humble and obedient servant'. The word 'remain' can be replaced with 'be' if desired.

In the body of the letter 'Your Royal Highness' should be substituted for 'you' and 'Your Royal Highness's' for 'your'.

The envelope should be addressed to 'His/Her Royal Highness' followed on the next line by the name:

The Prince Philip, Duke of Edinburgh, KG, KT, OM, GBE, AC, QSO, PC
The Prince of Wales, KG, KT, GCB, OM, AK, QSO, PC
The Prince William of Wales
The Prince Henry of Wales
The Duke of York, KG, KCVO, CD
Princess Beatrice of York
Princess Eugenie of York
The Earl of Wessex, KCVO
The Princess Royal, LG, LT, GCVO, QSO
The Duke of Gloucester, KG, GCVO
The Duke of Kent, KG, GCMG, GCVO
Prince Michael of Kent, GCVO
Princess Alexandra, The Hon Lady Ogilvy, LG, GCVO

Note: the postnominal letters listed are specific to the individual member of the Royal Family, i.e. not every Prince of Wales will have the same letters after the name.

Orders of Chivalry are accorded to members of the Royal Family, with the exception of the Queen.

VERBAL ADDRESS

'Your Royal Highness' for the first time and subsequently 'Sir' or 'Ma'am' as appropriate.

Pronunciation should be a normal 'Sir' and 'Ma'am' to rhyme with 'Pam'. 'Sire' is now archaic and should not be used.

INTRODUCTION

On introduction, a bow or curtsy is made.

The formal method of introduction was the invariable practice in the past, but many members of the Royal Family, particularly those of the younger generation, prefer a more informal method.

If there is any doubt concerning the degree of formality preferred by a member of the Royal Family an enquiry should be made to the respective private secretary, equerry or lady-in-waiting.

Even when an informal method is adopted a member of the Royal Family should always be addressed in conversation as 'Your Royal Highness' in the first instance and subsequently as 'Sir' or 'Ma'am'.

References to other members of the Royal Family are made to 'His (or Her) Royal Highness' or more informally, by the appropriate title, such as the Duke of Edinburgh or Princess Royal.

When introducing another person to a member of the Royal Family it is only necessary to state the name of the person to be introduced: 'May I present John Smith, Your Royal Highness?'

OFFICIAL FUNCTIONS

At official functions a speech should start 'Your Royal Highness(es)'. 'Sir' or 'Ma'am' may be used during the speech.

The Peerage

The peerage consists of the following groups:

(i)   Peer: of five grades, duke, marquess, earl, viscount and baron

(ii)   Peeress: duchess, marchioness, countess, viscountess and baroness, either in her own right or the wife or widow of a peer

(iii)   Courtesy lord: son and heir apparent of a duke, marquess and earl; eldest son of the heir apparent

(iv)   Wife or widow of a courtesy lord

(v)   The other sons of a peer with the courtesy style of Lord or The Honourable (usually abbreviated to Hon) before the forename, that is: younger sons of a duke and marquess (Lord John Brown), younger sons of an earl and all sons of a viscount or baron (The Hon John Brown)

(vi)   Sons of a courtesy lord, who have courtesy styles following the system mentioned in Group (v)

(vii)   Wives or sons of a peer or courtesy lord

(viii) Daughters of a peer, that is: daughters of a duke, marquess and earl (Lady Mary Brown) and daughters of a viscount and baron (The Hon Mary Brown or The Hon Mrs Brown)

(ix)   Daughters of a courtesy lord, who follow the same system mentioned in group (viii)

Though popularly known as the peerage, technically this can be divided into five separate peerages: the peerage of England, of Scotland, of Ireland, of Great Britain and of the United Kingdom. These terms are used in the technical sense of creation only and do not imply nationality. That is, the holder of an Irish peerage title is not necessarily from Ireland.

THE PEERAGE OF SCOTLAND
In the peerage of Scotland there is no rank of Baron, since in Scotland this term concerns a barony of land. The equivalent rank of Baron in the peerage of Scotland is Lord of Parliament, shortened to Lord.

TERRITORIAL DESIGNATION
Every viscount, baron and baroness is described in his or her letters patent of creation as being of a place in the United Kingdom, followed by the appropriate county. For example, Baron Redmayne of Rushcliffe in the county of Nottingham.

The place may be a residence, birthplace or some other location with which the peer has a connection. War leaders frequently embody the name of their battles or campaigns in their titles.

Such description is called the territorial designation and is not used, except in very formal documents.

A few peers have two territorial designations, of which at least one must be of a place in the United Kingdom: for example, Baron Wilson of Libya and of Stowlangtoft in the county of Suffolk.

An increasing number of peers have a territorial or place name that forms part of their title, such as Baron Bingham of Cornhill. Titles such as these should be used in full.

This territorial part of the peerage may be granted as a special honour, for example the late Earl Mountbatten of Burma, or else as a method of differentiation from the title of another peer.

This is particularly prevalent now that surnames, particularly for life peers, are adopted as peerage titles. For example, Baron Sainsbury of Turville and Baron Sainsbury of Preston Candover.

Differentiation may also be necessary if the first part of the title sounds like another existing peerage, even though the spelling may vary: Baron Hylton and Baron Hilton of Upton, Baron Layton and Baron Leighton of St Mellons.

HEIR APPARENT

The heir apparent to a dignity is either the eldest son, the eldest surviving son (where a deceased elder brother has left no heir apparent) or the only son of the holder of a dignity. When the heir apparent is deceased, his heir apparent succeeds him in this respect.

HEIR PRESUMPTIVE

The heir presumptive to a dignity is the next in line who could be displaced in succession by the birth of an heir apparent.

Thus a relative of a peer is only his heir presumptive until such time as the peer has a son and heir apparent.

HEIRESS PRESUMPTIVE

Alternatively, when a dignity may pass in the female line, the holder's daughter is heiress presumptive until such time as a son is born.

If there is more than one daughter, but no son, they are co-heirs to an English Barony, created by writ of summons.

Duke

A duke is always so described, unlike the lower ranks of the peerage. If reference is made to only one duke he may be called 'the Duke' but if distinction is necessary, or on introduction, he should be referred to as 'the Duke of Surrey'.

The style of The Most Noble has given way to His Grace in formal usage, but is still used occasionally in official announcements, documents and on monuments.

Ecclesiastical, ambassadorial and armed forces ranks precede ducal rank. For example, Major-General the Duke of Surrey.

The signature of a duke is by title only: Surrey.

WIFE OF A DUKE The wife of a duke is always described as the Duchess, or the Duchess of… if distinction is required.

The signature of a duchess is by forename and title: Helen Middlesex.

WIDOW OF A DUKE The widow of a duke is officially known as The Dowager Duchess of…, unless there is already a dowager duchess in that family still living. In the latter event, the widow of the senior duke retains the style of dowager for life, and the widow of the junior duke is known by her forename. For example, Ann, Duchess of Surrey.

Many widows do, however, prefer to use their forename. In the past, this was often announced in the press but this practice has fallen out of favour. It is therefore necessary to ascertain the wishes of the widow. If in doubt, the use of the forename is recommended.

If the present holder of the dukedom is unmarried, the widow of the previous duke continues to be known as the duchess. Should the present duke subsequently marry it is usual for the widowed duchess to then announce her preferred style.

FORMER WIFE OF A DUKE If a marriage to a duke has been dissolved, his former wife continues to use her title as a duke's wife, preceded by her forename: that is, Henrietta, Duchess of Surrey. She is not entitled to the formal prefix of Her Grace.

| | REMARRIAGE | Upon remarriage the former wife of a duke adopts her style from her new husband. |
| | | |

REMARRIAGE Upon remarriage the former wife of a duke adopts her style from her new husband.

If she has a courtesy style from her father she reverts to this upon remarriage, provided she does not marry another peer.

SCOTLAND In Scotland, a former wife is legally equivalent to a widow in English law. To this end, should the former wife of a duke remarry, she may retain her first husband's title as an alias.

	SALUTATION	ENVELOPE	VERBAL ADDRESS	CONVERSATION
Duke (formal)	My Lord Duke	His Grace the Duke of Surrey	Your Grace	The Duke or The Duke of Surrey
Duke (social)	Dear Duke	The Duke of Surrey	Duke	The Duchess or The Duchess of Surrey
Duchess (formal)	Madam or Dear Madam	Her Grace the Duchess of Surrey	Your Grace	The Duchess or The Duchess of Surrey
Duchess (social)	Dear Duchess	The Duchess of Surrey	Duchess	The Duchess or The Duchess of Surrey
Widowed Duchess	Dear Duchess	The Dowager Duchess of Surrey or Ann, Duchess of Surrey	Duchess	The Duchess or The Dowager Duchess of Surrey or Ann, Duchess of Surrey
Former Wife of a Duke	Dear Duchess	Henrietta, Duchess of Surrey	Duchess	The Duchess of Surrey or Ann, Duchess of Surrey
Eldest Son of a Duke	Courtesy title	Courtesy title	Courtesy title	Courtesy title
Younger Son of a Duke	Dear Lord Edward	Lord Edward FitzGerald	Lord Edward	Lord Edward
Wife of a Younger Son of a Duke	Dear Lady Edward	Lady Edward FitzGerald	Lady Edward	Lady Edward
Daughter of a Duke	Dear Lady Mary	Lady Mary FitzGerald	Lady Mary	Lady Mary

Marquess

The official spelling of the title is marquess, and is adopted in the Roll of the House of Lords, although the incorrect 'marquis' is frequently seen. In the past, when spelling was not standardised, both forms were used in Britain. Some Scottish marquesses, in memory of the 'Auld Alliance' with France, prefer the French spelling.

A marquess is, in conversation, referred to as Lord Twickenham rather than the Marquess of Twickenham. The exact rank is, however, used on envelopes, visiting cards and invitations.

Ecclesiastical, ambassadorial and armed forces ranks precede a marquess's rank: for example, Major-General the Marquess of Twickenham.

The signature of a marquess is by title only: Twickenham.

WIFE OF A MARQUESS	The wife of a marquess is a marchioness, and is known as Lady Twickenham. The use of her exact rank in speech is socially incorrect, unless it needs to be specifically mentioned, for example in a formal introduction.
	Her signature is by forename and title: Elizabeth Twickenham.
WIDOW OF A MARQUESS	The widow of a marquess is officially known as The Dowager Marchioness of… unless there is already a dowager marchioness in that family still living. In the latter event, the widow of the senior marquess retains the style of dowager for life and the widow of the junior marquess is known by her forename. For example, Elizabeth, Marquess of Twickenham.
	Many widows do, however, prefer to use their forename. In the past, this was often announced in the press but this practice has fallen out of favour. It is therefore necessary to ascertain the wishes of the widow. If in doubt, the use of the forename is recommended.
	If the present holder of the title is unmarried, the widow of the previous marquess continues to be known as the Marchioness. Should the present marquess subsequently marry it is usual for the widowed marchioness to then announce her preferred style.
FORMER WIFE OF A MARQUESS	If a marriage to a marquess has been dissolved his former wife continues to use her title of marchioness, preceded by her forename: that is, Henrietta, Marchioness of Twickenham. She is not entitled to the formal prefix of The Most Hon.

REMARRIAGE	Upon remarriage she adopts her style from her new husband. If she has a courtesy style from her father she reverts to this upon remarriage, provided she does not marry another peer.			
SCOTLAND	In Scotland, a former wife is legally equivalent to a widow in English law. To this end, should the former wife of a marquess remarry she may retain the use of her first husband's title as an alias.			

	SALUTATION	ENVELOPE	VERBAL ADDRESS	CONVERSATION
Marquess (formal)	My Lord	The Most Hon the Marquess of Twickenham	Your Grace	Lord Twickenham
Marquess (social)	Dear Lord Twickenham	The Marquess of Twickenham	Duke	Lord Twickenham
Marchioness (formal)	Dear Madam or Madam	The Most Hon the Marchioness of Twickenham	Your Grace	Lady Twickenham
Marchioness (social)	Dear Lady Twickenham	The Marchioness of Twickenham	Duchess	Lady Twickenham
Widowed Marchioness	Dear Lady Twickenham	The Dowager Marchioness of Twickenham or Elizabeth, Marchioness of Twickenham	Duchess	Lady Twickenham or the Dowager Lady Twickenham
Former Wife of a Marchioness	Dear Lady Twickenham	Elizabeth, Marchioness of Twickenham	Duchess	Lady Twickenham or Elizabeth, Lady Twickenham
Eldest Son of a Marquess	Courtesy title	Courtesy title	Courtesy title	Courtesy title
Younger Son of a Marquess	Dear Lord John	Lord John Brown	Lord John	Lord John
Wife of a Younger Son of a Marquess	Dear Lady John	Lady John Brown	Lady John	Lady John
Daughter of a Marquess	Dear Lady Helen	Lady Helen Brown	Lady Helen	Lady Helen

Earl

An earl is, in conversation, referred to as Lord Tolworth rather than the Earl of Tolworth. The exact rank is, however, used on envelopes, visiting cards and invitations.

Ecclesiastical, ambassadorial and armed forces ranks precede an earl's rank. For example, Major-General the Earl Tolworth.

The signature of an earl is by title only: Tolworth.

COUNTESS IN HER OWN RIGHT	A number of earldoms can be inherited in the female line. A countess in her own right is addressed as for the wife of an earl. Her husband would derive no title or style from his wife.
WIFE OF AN EARL	The wife of an earl is a countess, but is known as Lady Tolworth. The use of her exact rank in speech is socially incorrect, unless it needs to be specifically mentioned, for example in a formal introduction.
	The sole exception to this is HRH the Countess of Wessex, who is always referred to as Countess.
	The wife of an earl's signature is by forename and title: Emily Tolworth.
WIDOW OF AN EARL	The widow of an earl is officially known as The Dowager Countess of… unless there is already a dowager countess in that family still living. In the latter event, the widow of the senior earl retains the style of dowager for life and the widow of the junior earl is known by her forename: for example, Elizabeth, Countess of Tolworth.
	Many widows do, however, prefer to use their forename.
	In the past, this was often announced in the press but this practice has fallen out of favour. It is therefore necessary to ascertain the wishes of the widow. If in doubt, the use of the forename is recommended.
FORMER WIFE OF AN EARL	If the present holder of the title is unmarried, the widow of the previous earl continues to be known as the Countess. Should the present earl subsequently marry, it is usual for the widowed countess to then announce her preferred style.

If a marriage to an earl has been dissolved his former wife continues to use her title of countess, preceded by her forename: that is, Henrietta, Countess of Tolworth. She is not entitled to the formal prefix of The Rt Hon.

REMARRIAGE   Upon remarriage she adopts her style from her new husband. If she has a courtesy style from her father she reverts to this upon remarriage, provided she does not marry another peer.

SCOTLAND   In Scotland, a former wife is legally equivalent to a widow in English law. To this end, should the former wife of an earl remarry she may retain her first husband's title as an alias.

	SALUTATION	ENVELOPE	VERBAL ADDRESS	CONVERSATION
Earl (formal)	My Lord	The Rt Hon the Earl of Tolworth	My Lord	Lord Tolworth
Earl (social)	Dear Lord Tolworth	The Earl of Tolworth	Lord Tolworth	Lord Tolworth
Countess (formal)	Dear Madam or Madam	The Rt Hon the Countess of Tolworth	Madam	Lady Tolworth
Countess (social)	Dear Lady Tolworth	The Countess of Tolworth	Lady Tolworth	Lady Tolworth
Widowed Countess	Dear Lady Tolworth	The Dowager Countess of Tolworth or Emily, Countess of Tolworth	Lady Tolworth	Lady Tolworth or the Dowager Lady Tolworth
Former Wife of an Earl	Dear Lady Tolworth	Emily, Countess of Tolworth	Lady Tolworth	Lady Tolworth or Emily, Lady Tolworth
Eldest Son of an Earl	Courtesy title	Courtesy title	Courtesy title	Courtesy title
Younger Son of an Earl	Dear Mr Robinson	The Hon James Robinson	Mr Robinson (or appropriate rank)	Mr Robinson (or appropriate rank)
Wife of a Younger Son of an Earl	Dear Mrs Robinson	The Hon Mrs James Robinson	Mrs Robinson	Mrs Robinson
Daughter of an Earl	Dear Lady Elizabeth	Lady Elizabeth Robinson	Lady Elizabeth	Lady Elizabeth

Viscount

A viscount is, in conversation, referred to as Lord Frimley rather than the Viscount Frimley. The exact rank is, however, used on envelopes, visiting cards and invitations.

Ecclesiastical, ambassadorial and ranks of the Armed Forces precede a viscount's rank. For example, Major-General the Viscount Frimley.

The signature of a viscount is by title only: Frimley.

WIFE OF A VISCOUNT

The wife of a viscount is a viscountess but is known as Lady Frimley. The use of her exact rank in speech is socially incorrect, unless it needs to be specifically mentioned, for example in a formal introduction.

Her signature is by forename and title: Helen Frimley.

WIDOW OF A VISCOUNT

The widow of a viscount is officially known as The Dowager Viscountess... unless there is already a dowager viscountess in that family still living. In the latter event, the widow of the senior viscount retains the style of dowager for life and the widow of the junior viscount is known by her forename: for example, Helen, Viscountess Frimley.

Many widows do, however, prefer to use their forename.

In the past, this was often announced in the press but this practice has fallen out of favour. It is therefore necessary to ascertain the wishes of the widow. If in doubt, the use of the forename is recommended.

If the present holder of the title is unmarried, the widow of the previous viscount continues to be known as the Viscountess.

Should the present viscount subsequently marry it is usual for the widowed viscountess to then announce her preferred style.

FORMER WIFE OF A VISCOUNT

If a marriage to a viscount has been dissolved his former wife continues to use her title of viscountess, preceded by her forename. That is, Helen, Viscountess Tolworth.

She is not entitled to the formal prefix of The Rt Hon.

REMARRIAGE	Upon remarriage she adopts her style from her new husband.		

If she has a courtesy style from her father she reverts to this upon remarriage, provided she does not marry another peer.

SCOTLAND   In Scotland, a former wife is legally equivalent to a widow in English law.

To this end, should the former wife of a viscount remarry she may retain her first husband's title as an alias.

	SALUTATION	ENVELOPE	VERBAL ADDRESS	CONVERSATION
Viscount (formal)	My Lord	The Rt Hon the Viscount Frimley	My Lord	Lord Frimley
Viscount (social)	Dear Lord Frimley	The Viscount Frimley	Lord Frimley	Lord Frimley
Viscountess (formal)	Dear Madam or Madam	The Rt Hon the Viscountess Frimley	Madam	Lady Frimley
Viscountess (social)	Dear Lady Frimley	The Viscount Frimley	Lady Frimley	Lady Frimley
Widowed Viscountess	Dear Lady Frimley	The Dowager Viscountess of Frimley or Helen, Viscountess Frimley	Lady Frimley	Lady Frimley or the Dowager Lady Frimley
Former Wife of a Viscount	Dear Lady Frimley	Helen, Viscountess Frimley	Lady Frimley	Lady Frimley or Helen, Lady Frimley
Son of a Viscount	Dear Mr Grey	The Hon Robert Grey	Mr Grey (or appropriate rank)	Mr Grey (or appropriate rank)
Wife of a Son of a Viscount	Dear Mrs Grey	The Hon Mrs Robert Grey	Mrs Grey	Mrs Grey
Daughter of a Viscount	Dear Miss Grey or Dear Mrs Grey	The Hon Mary Grey (unmarried ladies only) or The Hon Mrs Grey	Miss Grey or Mrs Grey	Miss Grey or Mrs Grey

Baron

A baron is always referred to, both verbally and in correspondence, as Lord Hampton rather than Baron Hampton. The exact rank is never used, except in legal or formal documents. In the peerage of Scotland, the fifth grade of the peerage is a Lord (Lord of Parliament) in any case.

Ecclesiastical, ambassadorial and armed forces ranks precede a baron's rank: for example, Major-General the Lord Hampton.

The signature of a baron is by title only: Hampton.

BARONESS IN HER OWN RIGHT

A number of baronies can be inherited in the female line, and there are a large number of female life baronesses. A baroness in her own right is addressed as for the wife of a baron. She can decide whether to adopt the continental style of Baroness Molesey or else the more traditional Lady Molesey. In the peerage of Scotland Lady of Parliament is used, shortened to Lady. In both cases her husband would derive no title or style from his wife

Her signature is by title only: Molesey.

WIFE OF A BARON

The wife of a baron is known as Lady Hampton and the use of her exact rank in speech is socially incorrect, unless it needs to be specifically mentioned, for example in a formal introduction.

Her signature is by forename and title: Fiona Hampton.

WIDOW OF A BARON

The widow of a baron is officially known as The Dowager Lady… unless there is already a dowager baroness in that family still living. In the latter event, the widow of the senior baron retains the style of dowager for life and the widow of the junior baron is known by her forename: for example, Fiona, Lady Hampton.

Many widows do, however, prefer to use their forename in any case. In the past, this was often announced in the press but this practice has rather fallen out of favour. It is therefore necessary to ascertain the wishes of the widow. If in doubt, the use of the forename is recommended.

If the present holder of the title is unmarried, the widow of the previous baron continues to be known as the Baroness (or Lady). Should the present baron subsequently marry it is usual for the widowed baroness to then announce her preferred style.

FORMER WIFE OF A BARON If a marriage to a baron has been dissolved his former wife continues to use her title of baroness (or lady), preceded by her forename. That is, Fiona, Lady Hampton. She is not entitled to the formal prefix of The Rt Hon.

REMARRIAGE Upon remarriage she adopts her style from her new husband. If she has a courtesy style from her father she reverts to this upon remarriage.

SCOTLAND In Scotland, a former wife is legally equivalent to a widow in English law; should the former wife of a baron remarry, she may retain her first husband's title as an alias.

	SALUTATION	ENVELOPE	VERBAL ADDRESS	CONVERSATION
Baron (formal)	My Lord	The Rt Hon the Lord Hampton	My Lord	Lord Hampton
Baron (social)	Dear Lord Hampton	The Lord Hampton	Lord Hampton	Lord Hampton
Baroness (formal)	Dear Madam or Madam	The Rt Hon the Baroness (or Lady) Molesey	Madam	Lady Molesey
Baroness (social)	Dear Baroness Molesey or Dear Lady Molesey	The Baroness (or Lady) Molesey	Baroness Molesey or Lady Molesey	Lady Molesey
Widowed Baroness	Dear Lady Hampton	The Dowager Lady Hampton or Helen, Baroness Hampton	Lady Hampton	Lady Hampton or the Dowager Lady Hampton
Former Wife of a Baron	Dear Lady Hampton	Helen, Viscountess Hampton	Lady Hampton	Lady Hampton or Helen, Lady Hampton
Son of a Baron	Dear Mr Green	The Hon David Green	Mr Green (or appropriate rank)	Mr Green (or appropriate rank)
Wife of a Son of a Baron	Dear Mrs Green	The Hon Mrs David Green	Mrs Green	Mrs Green
Daughter of a Baron	Dear Miss Green or Dear Mrs Green	The Hon Mary Green (unmarried ladies only) or The Hon Mrs Green	Miss Green or Mrs Green	Miss Green or Mrs Green

Courtesy Titles and Styles

The children of a peer use either a peerage title by courtesy, or a courtesy style.

COURTESY STYLES Courtesy styles, as held by the daughters and younger sons of a duke, marquess or earl, and all daughters and sons of a viscount or baron, are listed in the tables on the preceding pages.

A peer's sons and daughters who are legitimated under the Legitimacy Act 1926, as amended by the Act of 1959, are now, under an Earl Marshal's Warrant, accorded the same courtesy styles as the legitimate younger children of peers, though they usually have no right of succession to the peerage or precedence from it.

Under Earl Marshal's Warrant 2004 the adopted children of a peer are accorded the courtesy titles that are proper to the younger children of peers, but without any rights of succession to that peerage.

BEARERS OF PEERAGE TITLES BY COURTESY A courtesy title indicates and reflects a legal right of precedence, unless in particular cases they are confirmed or recognised by the Sovereign. The eldest (or only) son and heir apparent of a duke, marquess or earl may use one of his father's peerage titles by courtesy, providing it is of a lesser grade than that used by his father.

This is usually, but not invariably, the second senior peerage borne by the peer. For example: the son and heir apparent of the Duke of Rutland is known as the Marquess of Granby.

When a marquess or earl by courtesy has an eldest (or only) son (who consequently is the second heir apparent), he, too, may use a courtesy title in the peerage, provided that it is junior in rank to that by which his father is known.

When the heir apparent of a duke, marquess or earl is deceased, but has left a son (who then becomes the heir apparent to the peer), he is allowed to use the courtesy title borne by his father.

If the eldest son of a viscount or baron predeceases his father, his children do not use the courtesy style of The Honourable. Thus the late Lord Kingsale, who succeeded his grandfather, did not have the style of The Honourable when his grandfather was the peer.

ADDRESSING BEARERS OF PEERAGE TITLES BY COURTESY

Though the bearer of a peerage title by courtesy enjoys none of the privileges of a peer, he is addressed as such with the following exceptions:

A marquess by courtesy is not given the formal style of The Most Hon.

An earl, viscount or baron by courtesy is not given the formal style of The Rt Hon.

A peer by courtesy is not addressed as 'The' in correspondence; this is restricted to actual peers.

Normally he is called Lord Blank, but if there is a special reason for a Marquess or Earl by courtesy to be referred to by his exact courtesy title, he is called verbally 'the Marquess of Blandford' or 'the Earl of Burford', this being the usual colloquial form of reference. The definite article is never given to courtesy viscounts and barons.

WIFE OF A PEER BY COURTESY

The wife of a peer by courtesy is addressed as the wife of a peer of the same rank, but with the following exceptions:

The wife of a marquess by courtesy is not given the formal style of The Most Hon.

The wife of an earl, viscount or baron by courtesy is not given the formal style of The Rt Hon.

The wife of a peer by courtesy is not given the prefix 'The' in correspondence.

WIDOW OF A PEER BY COURTESY

The widow of a peer by courtesy is addressed as the widow of a peer of the identical rank, with the above exceptions.

If the courtesy title has passed to her late husband's brother or other relation, she would prefix her title by her first name.

If it has passed to her son or stepson, she would prefix the title by her first name when he marries.

FORMER WIFE

She is styled as the former wife of a peer, other than a duke.

Other Titles & Styles

Baronet

A baronetcy is an hereditary dignity, the holder of which is accorded the prefix of Sir and the suffix of Baronet to his name. The suffix is invariably abbreviated in correspondence: Bt is usual, but the more old-fashioned Bart is sometimes preferred.

Scottish baronets sometimes use their territorial titles in conjunction with their surnames. In this case, Bt should appear at the end. For example, Sir John Macmillan of Lochmillan, Bt.

Ecclesiastical, armed forces and ambassadorial ranks should precede Sir: for example, The Rev Sir John Pelham, Bt.

Any postnominal letters follow Bt.

BARONETESS   If a woman inherits a baronetcy she is known as a baronetess with the prefix of Dame and the suffix Btss.

WIFE OF A BARONET   The wife of a baronet has the style of Lady before her surname or, for the wives of some Scottish baronets, the surname and territorial style.

The old-fashioned style of Dame followed by her forenames and surname is no longer in general use. It is, however, retained for legal documents.

It is useful for these purposes in that it allows for the identification of a particular person by the use of the forenames; an alternative legal style is for the forenames to be placed before Lady, e.g. Helen Lady Black.

Where confusion with others of the same surname could arise Lady may be followed by the forename in brackets, e.g. Lady (Helen) Black. This form is often used in publications.

If a baronet's wife has a courtesy style of Lady this is used in full e.g. Lady Helen Black. Similarly, the courtesy style of The Hon would precede the style of Lady from her marriage to a baronet e.g. The Hon Lady Black.

	WIDOW OF A BARONET
WIDOW OF A BARONET	Officially, the widow of a baronet immediately becomes a dowager on the death of her husband unless the widow of a senior baronet of the same creation is still alive. In this instance she would adopt her forename before the style of Lady.

Many dowagers prefer this latter style, so the wishes of the woman concerned should be ascertained. If in doubt, use the style of May, Lady Pelham. Should she remarry, she would take her style from her new husband.

When a baronet is unmarried the widow of his predecessor customarily continues to use the same style as when her husband was living. Should the present baronet subsequently marry it is usual for the widow of his predecessor to announce the style by which she wishes to be known.

In the case of widows who would have succeeded to a baronetcy had their husbands survived, the Queen may issue a Royal Warrant, by which the lady concerned may enjoy the same title, rank, place, pre-eminence and precedence as if her late husband had survived and succeeded to the title. This privilege is usually granted only when her late husband died in active service. |
| **FORMER WIFE OF A BARONET** | The former wife of a baronet has the style of her forename before Lady, provided she does not remarry. |
| **CHILDREN OF A BARONET** | The children of a baronet do not have any special style, but follow the rules for addressing untitled ladies or gentlemen. Children who have been adopted are not in line of succession to a baronetcy by reason of such adoption. |

	SALUTATION	ENVELOPE	VERBAL ADDRESS	CONVERSATION
Baronet	Dear Sir John	Sir John Pelham, Bt	Sir John	Sir John or Sir John Pelham
Baronetess	Dear Dame Alice	Dame Alice Hutton, Btss	Dame Alice	Dame Alice or Dame Alice Hutton
Wife of a Baronet	Dear Lady Pelham	Lady Pelham	Lady Pelham	Lady Pelham
Widow of a Baronet	Dear Lady Pelham	Dowager Lady Pelham or May, Lady Pelham	Lady Pelham	Lady Pelham or May, Lady Pelham
Former Wife of a Baronet	Dear Lady Pelham	May, Lady Pelham	Lady Pelham	Lady Pelham or May, Lady Pelham

Knight

The dignity of knighthood is the one most frequently conferred. It carries the prefix of Sir and is held for life. Knighthoods are not hereditary.

There are two types of knighthood conferred by the Sovereign: knights of the various orders of chivalry, identified by the appropriate letters after the name, and knights bachelor, which in ordinary correspondence carry no letters after the name.

The recipient is allowed to use the prefix Sir and also the appropriate letters for those orders of chivalry from the date of the announcement in the *London Gazette*: he does not wait for the accolade to be conferred upon him.

CLERGY	Ecclesiastical, armed forces and ambassadorial ranks should precede Sir: for example, His Excellency Sir Malcolm Edwards, KCMG.
	If a clergyman of the Church of England is subsequently appointed a knight of an order of chivalry he is not accorded the prefix of Sir, but he does place the appropriate letters after his name. For example, The Rt Rev the Bishop of Westerham, KCVO.
	Clergy of other churches may receive the accolade and thus the title Sir.
	A knight of an order of chivalry who is subsequently ordained a clergyman of the Church of England has no need to relinquish the prefix of Sir.
PEERS	A peer who receives a knighthood of an order of chivalry adds the appropriate letters of the order after his name. For example, the Viscount Angmering, KCVO.
HONORARY KNIGHTHOODS	When a foreign national receives an honorary knighthood of an order of chivalry he is not entitled to the prefix Sir, but he may place the appropriate letters after his name. For example, Spike Milligan, KBE.
	Should he subsequently become a naturalised British subject he will be entitled to receive the accolade.
	Having become a full knight of the appropriate order he will then use Sir before his name.

ORDERS OF CHIVALRY	The two senior orders of chivalry, the Order of the Garter and the Order of the Thistle, are exclusive and consist of one class only.

They carry the following letters after the name: KG (Knight of the Garter) and KT (Knight of the Thistle). Ladies of these orders carry the letters LG and LT.

The remaining orders of chivalry consist of several classes, of which the first two carry knighthoods: Knight Grand Cross or Knight Grand Commander, and Knight Commander.

There is no difference in the form of address for these types of knighthood. In both cases the appropriate letters are placed after the name.

USE OF POSTNOMINAL LETTERS

Should a knight be promoted within an order, he ceases to use the titles of his lower rank. For example, if Sir John Brown, KCB is raised to a GCB, he becomes Sir John Brown, GCB.

The same applies to a knight of an order of chivalry who previously belonged to the same order but of a class that did not carry a knighthood.

POSTNOMINAL LETTERS DENOTING KNIGHTHOODS OF ORDERS OF CHIVALRY

	KNIGHT GRAND CROSS OR KNIGHT GRAND COMMANDER	KNIGHT COMMANDER
Order of the Bath	GCB	KCB
Order of the Star of India	GCSI	KCSI
Order of St Michael and St George	GCMG	KCMG
Order of the Indian Empire	GCIE	KCIE
Royal Victorian Order	GCVO	KCVO
Order of the British Empire	GBE	KBE

PRECEDENCE OF LETTERS

When a knight receives more than one order of the same class the letters appear in order of precedence of the orders concerned and not according to the date on which he received them.

When a knight receives more than one order of a different class, the higher grade of a junior order is placed before the lower grade of a senior order. For example, Lt-Gen Sir John Brown, GBE, KCMG, CB, CVO.

For further information, see the Orders and Decorations section (*pages 130 to 133*).

CORRESPONDENCE

Where a knight has received several Orders of Chivalry, all the appropriate letters must be included after his name in correspondence.

HONORARY KNIGHT OF AN ORDER OF CHIVALRY

An honorary knight of an order of chivalry uses the appropriate letters after his name, but without the prefix Sir because he is not eligible to receive the accolade.

KNIGHT BACHELOR

In legal and official documents, the suffix 'Knight' may be added after the name of a knight bachelor. In all other cases nothing comes after the name: the prefix Sir serves to indicate the knighthood.

Knighthood does not affect the use of letters already borne. If a Mr John Brown, CB, CVO, OBE, is created a knight bachelor, he becomes Sir John Brown, CB, CVO, OBE.

WIFE OF A KNIGHT

The wife of a knight is known as Lady, followed by her surname e.g. Lady Smith. The old-fashioned style of Dame followed by her forenames and surname is no longer in general use. It is, however, retained for legal documents.

It is useful for these purposes in that it allows for the identification of a particular person by the use of the forenames; an alternative legal style is for the forenames to be placed before Lady, e.g. Edith, Lady Smith.

Where confusion with others of the same surname could arise Lady may be followed by the forename in brackets, e.g. Lady (Edith) Smith. This form is often used in publications.

The wife of a knight should never be styled Lady Edith Smith, unless she is the daughter of a duke, marquess or earl, when she can be styled in this way.

100

COURTESY STYLES	If a knight's wife is the daughter of a viscount or baron and therefore bears the courtesy style of The Honourable, this precedes the style of Lady. She is styled as The Hon Lady Smith.	

COURTESY STYLES — If a knight's wife is the daughter of a viscount or baron and therefore bears the courtesy style of The Honourable, this precedes the style of Lady. She is styled as The Hon Lady Smith.

CLERGY — The wife of a Church of England clergyman who subsequently receives a knighthood continues to be addressed as Mrs John Smith, but she has the precedence of the wife of a knight.

WIFE OF AN HONORARY KNIGHT — The wife of an honorary knight continues to be addressed as Mrs John Smith.

WIDOW OR FORMER WIFE OF A KNIGHT — The widow of a knight is addressed as the wife of a knight, provided that she does not remarry. On remarriage she would take her style from her husband. This is also true of the former wife of a knight.

CHILDREN OF A KNIGHT — The children of a knight do not have any special style.

	SALUTATION	ENVELOPE	VERBAL ADDRESS	CONVERSATION
Knight Bachelor	Dear Sir John	Sir John Smith	Sir John	Sir John or Sir John Smith
GCB	Dear Sir John	Sir John Smith, GCB	Sir John	Sir John or Sir John Smith
GCSI	Dear Sir John	Sir John Smith, GCSI	Sir John	Sir John or Sir John Smith
GCIE	Dear Sir John	Sir John Smith, GCIE	Sir John	Sir John or Sir John Smith
GCVO	Dear Sir John	Sir John Smith, GCVO	Sir John	Sir John or Sir John Smith
GBE	Dear Sir John	Sir John Smith, GBE	Sir John	Sir John or Sir John Smith
KCB	Dear Sir John	Sir John Smith, KCB	Sir John	Sir John or Sir John Smith
KCSI	Dear Sir John	Sir John Smith, KCSI	Sir John	Sir John or Sir John Smith
KCIE	Dear Sir John	Sir John Smith, KCIE	Sir John	Sir John or Sir John Smith
KCVO	Dear Sir John	Sir John Smith, KCVO	Sir John	Sir John or Sir John Smith
KBE	Dear Sir John	Sir John Smith, KBE	Sir John	Sir John or Sir John Smith
Wife of a Knight	Dear Lady Smith	Lady Smith	Lady Smith	Lady Smith

Dame

A Dame is the female equivalent of a knight of an order of chivalry. It carries the prefix of Dame and is held for life. Damehoods are not hereditary.

The recipient is allowed to use this prefix and also the appropriate letters for those of orders of chivalry from the date of the announcement in the *London Gazette*. She does not wait for the accolade to be conferred upon her.

PEERESS AND COURTESY TITLES	A peeress who is appointed a dame, including a holder of a peerage title by courtesy, adds the appropriate letters after her name. For example, the Countess of Dorking, DCVO.
	A woman with the courtesy style of Lady would add the appropriate letters after her name, but not the prefix Dame.
	Those styled The Hon are addressed The Hon Dame Mary Jones, DBE.
ORDERS OF CHIVALRY	The orders of chivalry consist of several classes, of which the first two carry damehoods: Dame Grand Cross and Dame Commander. There is no difference in the form of address for these types of honour. In both cases the appropriate letters are placed after the name.
USE OF POSTNOMINAL LETTERS	Should a dame be promoted within an order, she ceases to use the titles of her lower rank. For example, if Dame Muriel Brown, DCB is raised to a GCB she becomes Dame Muriel Brown, GCB.
	The same applies to a dame of an order of chivalry who previously belonged to the same order but of a class that did not carry a damehood.

POSTNOMINAL LETTERS DENOTING ORDERS OF CHIVALRY		DAME GRAND CROSS	DAME COMMANDER
	Order of the Bath	GCB	DCB
	Order of St Michael and St George	GCMG	DCMG
	Royal Victorian Order	GCVO	DCVO
	Order of the British Empire	GBE	DBE

PRECEDENCE OF LETTERS	When a dame receives more than one order of the same class the letters appear in order of precedence of the orders concerned and not according to the date on which she received them.		
	For further information, see the Orders and Decorations section (*pages 130–133*).		
THE ORDER OF THE HOSPITAL OF ST JOHN OF JERUSALEM	Letters that signify membership of the Most Venerable Order of the Hospital of St John of Jerusalem are not included after the name. Dames Grand Cross and Dames of Justice of Grace of the order do not bear the prefix of Dame.		
PROFESSIONAL NAMES	When a dame of an order of chivalry is gazetted by her professional, rather than her legal, name she generally prefers to be so addressed: for example, Dame Margot Fonteyn, DBE rather than Dame Peggy Hookham, DBE.		
HUSBAND OF A DAME	The husband of a dame does not derive any title or style from his wife.		

	SALUTATION	ENVELOPE	VERBAL ADDRESS	CONVERSATION
GCB	Dear Dame Helen	Dame Helen Smith, GCB	Dame Helen	Dame Helen or Dame Helen Smith
GCVO	Dear Dame Helen	Dame Helen Smith, GCVO	Dame Helen	Dame Helen or Dame Helen Smith
GBE	Dear Dame Helen	Dame Helen Smith, GBE	Dame Helen	Dame Helen or Dame Helen Smith
DCB	Dear Dame Helen	Dame Helen Smith, DCB	Dame Helen	Dame Helen or Dame Helen Smith
DCVO	Dear Dame Helen	Dame Helen Smith, DCVO	Dame Helen	Dame Helen or Dame Helen Smith
DBE	Dear Dame Helen	Dame Helen Smith, DBE	Dame Helen	Dame Helen or Dame Helen Smith

Privy Counsellor

The Privy Council, the ancient executive governing body of the United Kingdom, is presided over by the Sovereign. It exercises many functions, some entrusted to it by Acts of Parliament, which may be legislative, administrative or judicial.

Its decisions are usually embodied in Orders in Council or Proclamations.

MEMBERSHIP

Membership is for life, with the style of 'Right Honourable'.

Privy counsellors are appointed by the Crown from persons distinguished in various walks of public life, at home and in the Commonwealth, including members of the Royal Family, the Archbishops of Canterbury and York, the Bishop of London, the Lord Chancellor, members of the judiciary, all Cabinet ministers and some overseas prime ministers. The Lord President of the Council is usually a senior member of the Cabinet.

NOTE ON SPELLING

The spelling 'privy councillor' is also used, but the Privy Council Office prefers the spelling 'counsellor'.

FORMS OF ADDRESS

There is no special form of address used when writing to a member of the Privy Council. Similarly, membership of the Privy Council does not affect verbal address or description in conversation in any way.

PEER OR PEERESS

He or she is addressed according to peerage rank, with the letters after the title and any orders. The letters PC follow all honours and decorations awarded by the Crown, as membership of the Privy Council is an appointment rather than a conferred honour.

OTHERS

The Rt Hon is always placed before the name in both formal and social usage. There is no need to add the letters PC after the name since the prefix is sufficient indication of membership of the Privy Council.

Other ranks, such as ecclesiastical, armed forces and ambassadorial, precede The Rt Hon. Women who are privy counsellors drop the use of Miss, Mrs or Ms.

SPOUSES

The spouses of privy counsellors acquire no title or style.

Untitled Persons

UNTITLED MEN   It is customary to be addressed as Mr John Brown. The use of just the forename and surname was once considered impolite but is now widely used, i.e. John Brown.

The use of 'Esq' – e.g. John Brown, Esq – is now antiquated and rarely used.

UNMARRIED WOMAN   An unmarried woman may be styled Miss or Ms, followed by her forename and surname. When a woman marries she may continue to use her maiden name. If she does, she should still be styled Miss unless she makes it clear that she prefers otherwise.

MARRIED WOMAN   While it was once customary only for a divorced woman to use her own forename with Mrs (Mrs Mary Brown), the practice is now widespread among married women and widows. Traditionally, married women and widows would use their husband's forename with Mrs (Mrs John Brown). This style can still be used and is appropriate for formal correspondence.

MS   In business, Ms is often used as a convenient female equivalent of Mr. It is, however, always advisable to find out if someone prefers to be styled as Miss, Mrs or Ms. Some women also prefer to be styled Ms in social situations.

	SALUTATION	ENVELOPE	VERBAL ADDRESS	CONVERSATION
Man	Dear Mr Brown	John Brown, Esq or Mr John Brown	Mr Brown	Mr Brown
Unmarried woman	Dear Miss Brown	Miss Emma Brown	Miss Brown	Miss Brown
Married woman or widow (see text)	Dear Mrs Brown	Mrs Mary Brown or Mrs John Brown	Mrs Brown	Mrs Brown
Divorced woman (see text)	Dear Mrs Brown	Mrs Mary Brown	Mrs Brown	Mrs Brown
Ms	Dear Ms Brown	Ms Sarah Brown	Ms Brown	Ms Brown

Joint Forms of Address

There are occasions when it may be fitting to use a joint form of address for a husband and wife, or other partnership, when addressing an envelope. Christmas cards and letters to close relatives and friends are the most obvious examples.

INVITATIONS

The use of the joint form for invitations to both public and private functions is also becoming common, although it is potentially very complicated. The former were traditionally addressed to the husband, if sent to his official address, and the latter to the wife at the home address.

Women are now guests in their own right on a more regular basis. Clearly, if the female partner in a relationship is being invited in her official capacity, while her husband is included as a courtesy, then the invitation should not be addressed to him alone.

Equally, many people feel that to address an invitation to a private function solely to a wife is somewhat old-fashioned and formal.

UNMARRIED COUPLES

There is often the need to address unmarried couples in the joint form. The only awkward consideration here might be the order in which to list the names.

If applicable, it is usually sensible to name first whichever partner is the 'official' invitee. In other cases, discretion and common sense must be the host's guides.

DOCTORS

A couple who are both doctors, when the wife practises under her maiden name, should still be addressed in the traditional social style of Dr and Mrs Cross.

In a professional capacity, however, they would of course be listed under their individual names.

CIVIL PARTNERSHIP

Same-sex couples who have registered a Civil Partnership are permitted to change or hyphenate their surnames to indicate their legal union. The Civil Partnership certificate is accepted as documentation allowing names to be changed names.

DIFFERENT STYLES   The chief difficulty in using a joint form arises where husband and wife are differently styled.

The following are some examples:

Formal: The Most Hon the Marquess and Marchioness of Bath
Social: The Marquess and Marchioness of Bath

Formal: The Rt Hon the Earl and Countess of Darlington
Social: The Earl and Countess of Darlington

Formal: The Rt Hon the Viscount and Viscountess of Falkland
Social: The Viscount and Viscountess Falkland

Formal: The Rt Hon the Lord and Lady Gretton
Social: The Lord and Lady Gretton

Sir Harry Callow, Bt and Lady Callow, OBE
The Hon George and Lady Moira Black
The Hon Guy and Mrs White
Mr John and Lady Barbara Jones
Mr John and the Hon Mrs Green
Mr Gerald Lytton and Dame Alice Lytton, DBE
Professor Sir Alexander Bright, MBE and Lady Bright
Lieutenant-Colonel the Hon John and Mrs Smith
Major John and the Hon Mrs Smith
HE Mr David Manners, CBE and Mrs Manners
Captain Andrew Taylor, RN and Mrs Taylor
The Reverend Canon Dr and Mrs Goodenough
Mr Alfred and Dr Mary Bannerman
Mr Frederick and Professor Janet Ramsay
The Worshipful Mayor of Northampton and the Lady Mayoress
The Worshipful Mayor of Worcester and Mr Brian Allingham
The Reverend John and Mrs Smith
Mr and Mrs Thomas Brown

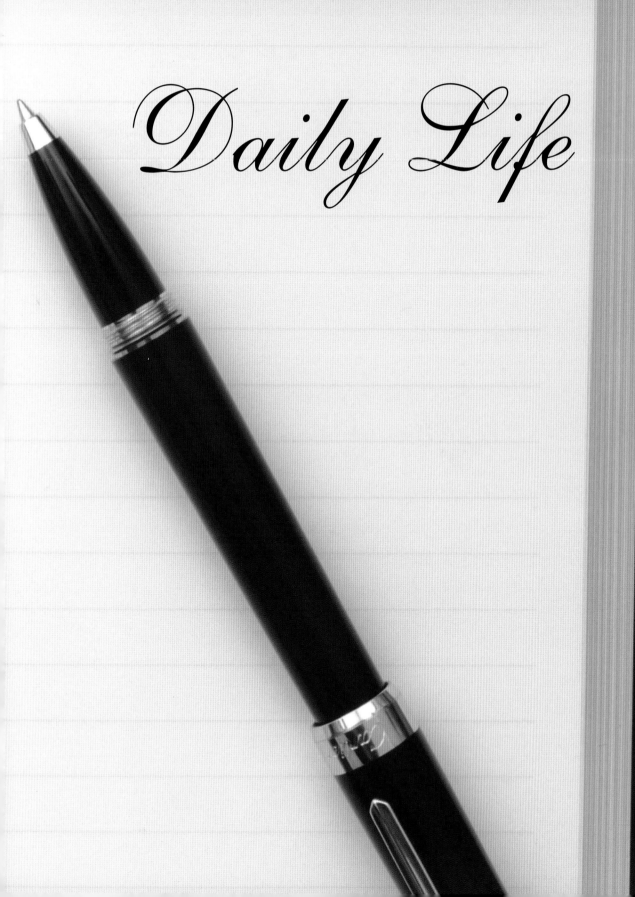

Daily Life

Letter Writing

The highest quality stationery must be used at all times. A modern, contemporary feel can be introduced to personalised stationery through unusual fonts or coloured inks.

WRITING PAPER

Writing paper should be white, ivory or cream, and a minimum weight of 100 gsm^2 to avoid show through.

Paper should always be plain; a lined undersheet can be used as a template. The traditional size is either 8 x 6$^1/_4$ inches (20 x 16 cm) or 7 x 5$^1/_2$ inches (18 x 14 cm).

LETTERHEAD

A letterhead should include the postal address, telephone number and, if desired, email address. Names are never included.

The very best, and most expensive, letterhead would have engraved lettering.

Flat printing is a more affordable alternative; thermography should be avoided unless of very high quality.

ENVELOPES

Envelopes should match the writing paper and always have diamond flaps. Postage stamps, not franking machines, should be used for personal correspondence.

CORRESPONDENCE CARDS

Correspondence cards should be postcard-sized and a minimum of 300 gsm^2. They include the name, address, telephone number and e-mail address.

When a postal address is not permanent, they can be printed with just a name, mobile telephone number and email address.

Correspondence cards are always sent in an envelope.

PRESTON TOWER
HILL OF FAYRE
ABERDEENSHIRE
TELEPHONE: 01786 47308

9th October 2006

Dear Christopher,

I hope you are well. It has been a very long time since we last managed to meet.

We have recently returned from a long three week holiday in Australia. I highly recommend you visit, Sydney and the Great Barrier Reef really are unmissable.

Jonathan has just gone off to university and soon Christmas will be here. We are visiting friends near Salisbury at the beginning of December, so we must try to meet up while we are in your neck of the woods.

I look forward to hearing your news.

With love

Sarah

Births & Ceremonies

COMMUNICATION OF THE BIRTH

The new father spreads the news of the birth, by telephone, to close family, future godparents and friends. This duty is often shared by a grandparent or other relative. If there are complications, the announcement may be delayed until the health or wellbeing of the mother and baby are known.

BIRTH ANNOUNCEMENT CARDS

Birth announcement cards should be printed or engraved and kept elegantly simple. Photographs of the new baby should never be sent out.

Samantha
31st May

ROBIN AND JENNIFER BIRD
are delighted to announce
the birth of their daughter, a sister for Henry

15 Lots Road
London SW10 0QJ

FORMAL BIRTH ANNOUNCEMENTS

Birth announcements, in local or national papers, are kept short and succinct. Other information, such as the mother's maiden name or news of delighted siblings, should not be included. A traditional announcement would read:

Campbell – On 20th August to John and Claire a son, Thomas Edward

In the case of unmarried parents, the surnames of the parents are included:

Campbell – On 20th August to John Campbell and Claire Bottomley
a son, Thomas Edward

In the case of single parents the announcement is simplified:

Bottomley – On 20th August to Claire a son, Thomas Edward

LETTERS OF CONGRATULATION	After the announcement, a short letter of congratulations should be sent to the parents, addressed to the mother, on writing paper or a correspondence card.
	A suitable greetings card or postcard can be sent where a group of people – e.g. work colleagues – wishes to congratulate the mother.
INVITATIONS TO BIRTH CEREMONIES	Christenings or baptisms do not usually require formal invitations. Notification to godparents, friends and family is made via personal notes or telephone calls. This will include invitations to any social gathering afterwards.
	The Jewish rites of brit milah and any private parties afterwards are made known through personal communication.
CONFIRMATION AND FIRST COMMUNION	It is usual to have a social gathering of friends, family and godparents after the ceremonies of confirmation and first communion (Roman Catholic).
	As they are intimate affairs, invitations may be given in person or in short handwritten notes.
BAR MITZVAH OR BAT MITZVAH	Printed or engraved invitations are sent out for formal receptions following bar mitzvah for boys and bat mitzvah for girls.
	The format for these is not dissimilar to a wedding invitation. They are issued by the parents, inviting the recipient to join in the ceremony of their son/daughter on a specified time and date at the synagogue, and to attend the reception afterwards at a home or another venue.
	Recipients should respond with a handwritten reply.
	For less formal celebrations, invitations may take the form of handwritten letters, notes or postcards, or be given in person.
ADOPTION CARDS	It has become more common to announce the adoption of a child. Cards can be sent out to friends and relatives. The wording would read:

Mr and Mrs Campbell wish to announce the arrival

of Thomas Edward into their lives

Engagement

It is customary for the parents of the engaged couple to spread the news to close family and friends, but the couple may choose make the announcement themselves.

**ENGAGEMENT
ANNOUNCEMENT**

A traditional engagement announcement is made in local or national papers and should read:

> Mr J Davenport and Miss P Smythe
>
> The engagement is announced between John,
>
> second son of Dr and Mrs Isaac Davenport
>
> of Jack's Bush, Wiltshire, and Patricia, only daughter
>
> of Mr and Mrs Peter Smythe of Piddletown, Dorset

If the bride-to-be is divorced, or one or both sets of parents are divorced, each parent and their address is clearly outlined:

> Mr J Davenport and Miss P Smythe (Ms or Mrs)
>
> The engagement is announced between John,
>
> second son of Dr Isaac Davenport of Jack's Bush, Wiltshire and
>
> Mrs Joan Davenport of London, and Patricia,
>
> only daughter of Mr Peter Smythe of Piddletown, Dorset
>
> and Mrs Sarah Anthony of Oban, Argyllshire

If one of the parents is widowed:

> Mr J Davenport and Miss P Smythe
>
> The engagement is announced between John, second son of
>
> Dr and Mrs Isaac Davenport
>
> of Jack's Bush, Wiltshire, and Patricia, only daughter
>
> of Mrs Peter Smythe of Piddletown, Dorset

The couple may wish to announce their engagement in a more contemporary style:

> Mr John Davenport of Pimlico London and Miss Patricia
>
> Smythe of Bournemouth, Dorset are delighted to announce
>
> their engagement, a summer wedding is planned

ENGAGEMENT PARTY	If a party is held to celebrate the engagement, the normal rules for invitations apply for formal engagement parties.
	It should be clearly noted on the invitation that the function is being held to mark this specific event.
LETTER OF CONGRATULATIONS	It is appropriate to write a letter to friends, colleagues and family upon hearing they have become engaged.
	This should be a handwritten letter; a congratulatory email or text should always be followed up by handwritten correspondence.
	It is still considered improper to congratulate the bride as it implies that she has 'caught her man'. It is, however, appropriate to congratulate the groom-to-be.
SAVE THE DATE CARDS	Many couples send a printed card prior to the wedding invitation asking potential guests to keep a particular date free to attend the ceremony.
	If further details are confirmed, more information can be included, such as the actual name of the church or venue.
	The wording is simple and brief. For example:

Please Save the Date
for the marriage of
John Davenport and Patricia Smythe
Saturday 13th May 2006
London
Invitation to follow

WEDDING ANNOUNCEMENTS	Wedding announcements are often published in the local and national press shortly after the ceremony. This public announcement is usually simple and to the point:

Mr J Davenport and Miss(Mrs/Ms) P Smyth [other titles as appropriate]
The marriage took place at St Barnabas Church, Piddletown, Dorset
on 13th May between Mr John Davenport (of Pimilco)
and Miss Patricia Smyth of (Bournemouth)

Bereavement

The news of a death should be broken face-to-face, or on the telephone. More distant relatives and friends may be told by letter. The news must never be communicated by email or text message.

COMMUNICATION OF THE DEATH

The public announcement of the bereavement and details of the funeral and/or memorial service are usually published in a death notice placed by the family in local or national newspapers.

DEATH NOTICES

An announcement is made in local or national papers. They vary in length, but should be kept simple and to the point.

Essential details include the name of the deceased, residence (town or village), date of death and any special arrangements.

Where and when services will be held, whether to send flowers and the charity donations are being sent to are often included.

LETTERS OF CONDOLENCE

A letter of condolence should be sent promptly after the death announcement. It should be well thought out, and appropriate to the relationship with the deceased or the family.

The letter should be always be handwritten (never be typed or sent via email) addressed to the spouse or the next of kin (son or daughter), and be posted first class or delivered by hand.

A response to letters of sympathy and condolence is not necessary and should never be expected.

THANK YOU LETTERS

Those closely involved in the funeral arrangements, such as the pallbearers or speakers, or those who have given flowers and gifts, should be acknowledged.

This can be done in a simple short handwritten note thanking them for their time and contribution to the day.

9th September
2006

Dear Charles,

I was extremely sorry to hear that Agatha has died. She shall be greatly missed.

My thoughts are with you all.

With love

Sarah

Thank You Letters

A handwritten thank you letter is always appreciated. As a general rule, a thank you letter should be written within a week to ten days of an event or receipt of a present.

The form of the invitation signals the appropriate format of a thank you. Engraved invitation cards require a formal thank you letter. An At Home card suggests a short letter or note.

FORMAL THANK YOU LETTERS	A formal thank you letter should be handwritten and sent by post, usually first class, or delivered by hand. Traditionally addressed to the hostess, nowadays they can be addressed to either the host, hostess or couple as appropriate. Formal thank you letters are necessary to acknowledge presents given for christenings, weddings, major birthdays and anniversaries.
INFORMAL THANK YOU LETTERS	Support during a key event or task – bereavement, wedding, reference for a job – should be acknowledged with a brief letter of thanks.
	Presents from close friends and family should be acknowledged by an informal note. A verbal, telephone or email invitation needs only a telephone call of thanks after the event; telephone and email are interchangeable if all parties use both frequently.
CHILDREN'S THANK YOU LETTERS	It is appropriate for parents to respond on behalf of their offspring before the child is able to write. The child should write their own, however, as soon as they can.

Max

Dear Granny,

Thank you for the camera. It is brilliant. I had a great birthday. I went to the Zoo with George and saw the elephants and the tigers.

George helped me take some photos. I will send them to you when they are printed.

I hope you are well.

Love
Max

THE LODGE HOUSE
LANGTON MALTRAVERS
DORSET BH21 OYE
TEL: 01725 843192
FAX: 01725 843193

20th September 2006

My dear Sylvia,

Thank you for a wonderful dinner: I haven't had so much fun in ages.

It was also a great treat to see Annabel after all this time, and your chocolate pudding was marvellous - I must get the recipe from you.

I hope you enjoy your trip to India, and look forward to returning hospitality when you get back.

With love

Sarah

Greetings Cards

Greetings cards must not be sent out to mark numerous trivial events, or when a letter is more appropriate.

Humorous cards should be avoided, unless the recipient is very well known. Simple motifs and messages are more appropriate. Electronic cards are impersonal, unreliable and inappropriate.

SPECIAL OCCASIONS

Greetings cards can be sent on birthdays and anniversaries, or for special occasions such as Mother's Day and Valentine's Day.

They are also appropriate as a congratulatory gesture to acquaintances or friends, e.g. to the son of a close friend who has graduated from university.

Cards are useful if a number of people wish to send a group message, e.g. a farewell card for a colleague who is leaving that has been signed by everyone in the office.

Cards should always be handwritten in ink. It is customary for the husband's name to be given before his wife's, but this is a matter of personal choice.

The wife's forename is, however, retained. Therefore, a card should be inscribed from 'John and Mary Smith', rather than from 'Mr and Mrs John Smith'.

CHRISTMAS CARDS

If Christmas cards are pre-printed, then the surname should be crossed through for recipients on first-name terms with the senders.

It is permissible to include a short personal letter when the card is to friends or relatives who are rarely seen. However, a general newsletter, or photographs of the family and pets, are not considered acceptable inclusions.

It is often wise to take care when sending cards to those of other faiths: to this end 'season's greetings' can be a more appropriate a greeting.

Christmas cards are a traditional expression of seasonal goodwill and the sending of cards should be in this spirit, rather than for personal promotion.

Christmas cards are traditionally sent in envelopes with diagonal flaps.

Change of Address

A card announcing a change of address should be sent out as soon as the essential details have been confirmed.

INFORMATION   The card should simply include the names of the sender(s), the new address and telephone number.

TIMING   A moving date is included if the card is being sent out in advance. Otherwise, the above information is sufficient.

ILLUSTRATED CARDS   A simple motif is acceptable; cards featuring photographs or illustrations of the new property are inappropriate.

CHANGE OF ADDRESS

CHRISTOPHER & JENNIFER WREN

CHELSEA HOUSE
CHEYNE WALK
LONDON SW3 5DX

TELEPHONE: 020 7352 7063
MOBILE: 07710 3526073
EMAIL: orders@wrenpress.com

Orders & Decorations

Letters after the Name

PRECEDENCE OF LETTERS

The abbreviations 'Bt' or 'Bart' for a baronet and 'Esq', if applicable, precede all other letters after the name. Other letters are grouped either by regulations or by custom, in the following order of precedence:

(i)   Orders and decorations conferred by the Crown

(ii)   Appointments in the following order:
Privy Counsellor	PC
Aide de Camp to The Queen	ADC
Honorary Physician to The Queen	QHP
Honorary Surgeon to The Queen	QHS
Honorary Dental Surgeon to The Queen	QHDS
Honorary Nursing Sister to The Queen	QHNS
Honorary Chaplain to The Queen	QHC

(iii)
Queen's Counsel	QC
Justice of the Peace	JP
Deputy Lieutenant	DL

(iv)   University degrees

(v)   Religious orders
         Medical qualifications

(vi)   Fellowships of learned societies
         Royal Academicians and Associates
         Fellowships, memberships etc. of professional bodies
         Writers to the Signet

(vii)   Member of Parliament   MP

(viii)   Membership of one of the Armed Forces

It is important to keep to the group order, even if the individual series of letters in groups (iv), (v) and (vi) present difficulties. For further information see the appropriate section below.

INCLUSION OF LETTERS

The nature of the correspondence determines which series of letters should normally be included under groups (iv), (v) and (vi).

For instance, when writing a professional letter to a doctor of medicine one would normally add more medical qualifications than in a social letter.

LISTS OF NAMES

On a formal list, all the appropriate letters are usually included after each name.

CROWN HONOURS

Those who have letters signifying Crown honours and awards are usually given only the principal letters in groups (iv), (v) and (vi). For example, MD, FRCS and FRS.

PEERS

A peer who is a junior officer in the Armed Forces is not usually addressed by his Service rank in social correspondence unless he so wishes, or a letter is forwarded to him at a Service address or club.

ORDERS AND DECORATIONS

All the appropriate letters are obligatory in correspondence and lists. The order is laid down in the section on knights, dames and others.

PRIVY COUNSELLORS AND APPOINTMENTS TO THE QUEEN

For peers the letters PC are obligatory. For other privy counsellors 'The Rt Hon' before the name is sufficient identification.

As the other appointments to the Crown, such as QHP and QHS, are held for a limited period only recipients do not always use them.

APPOINTMENTS

The letters QC are shown for a Queen's Counsel, except when the individual is also a High Court Judge.

The letters JP for Justice of the Peace and DL for a Deputy Lieutenant may be included in that order.

In practice they are often omitted for a peer, or for someone with several honours and awards.

There is no official abbreviation for a Lord-Lieutenant, HM Lieutenant or a Vice Lord-Lieutenant.

UNIVERSITY DEGREES	Doctorates in the Faculties of Divinity and Medicine (DD and MD) and Masters degrees in the latter (for example, MS) are given in all correspondence. Other divinity degrees, such as BD, are sometimes included.

Other degrees in medicine, such as MB or BS, are sometimes included, especially in professional correspondence, but if one progresses in the same degree only the higher is given.

Doctorates in other faculties are sometimes given, especially if the correspondence concerns the particular profession or subject.

Alternatively, and with the exception of surgeons, the envelope may be addressed with Doctor before the name, without giving the letters of the degree.

Other degrees are seldom, and MA and BA never, used in social correspondence, but they are generally included in a formal list.

RELIGIOUS ORDERS

Letters for members of religious communities, when used, should be included: SJ (Society of Jesus), for example.

Some members of the Order of St Benedict do not use the letters OSB, as the prefix of Dom or Dame is held to be a sufficient identification.

MEDICAL QUALIFICATIONS

Fellowships, such as FRCP and FRCS, are given in all correspondence.

Other qualifications are sometimes given, especially those which are the highest held. They are usually included when writing professionally.

ORDER OF LETTERS (MEDICAL)

When all letters signifying qualifications are included, as for example in a nominal list, they should appear in the following order: medicine; surgery (except MRCS); obstetrics, gynaecology and other specialities; qualifying diplomas, such as MRCS and LRCP; other diplomas, such as DPH, DObst, RCOT.

Fellows and members of each category precede the next category.

In practice, a maximum of three series of letters, including MD, is usually sufficient in ordinary correspondence.

FELLOWSHIPS OF LEARNED SOCIETIES

Fellowships fall into two categories: honorific – that is, nomination by election – and nomination by subscription. Normally only honorific fellowships are used in social correspondence, such as FRS or FBA.

Fellowships by subscription are generally restricted to correspondence concerning the same field of interest. For example, a writer to a fellow of the Zoological Society on the subject of zoology will include FZS after the name.

ORDER OF LETTERS (LEARNED SOCIETIES)

There is no recognised order for the placing of these letters. Strictly speaking, letters should be arranged according to the date of foundation or incorporation of the societies concerned, but some hold that those with a Royal Charter should take precedence.

In practice, where one society is indisputably of greater importance than another the letters are usually placed in that order. Alternatively, the fellowship of the junior society may be omitted. If such precedence cannot be determined, the letters may be placed in order of conferment. Where this is not known, they may be placed in alphabetical order.

Where a fellow is pre-eminent in a particular subject, the fellowship of a society connected with this interest may either be placed first or other fellowships omitted.

The following are some of the principal learned societies, with their dates of incorporation:

Fellow of the Royal Society	FRS	1662
Fellow of the Society of Antiquaries	FSA	1707
Fellow of the Royal Society of Edinburgh	FRSE	1783
Fellow of the Royal Society of Literature	FRSL	1823
Fellow of the British Academy	FBA	1901

PRESIDENTS OF LEARNED SOCIETIES

Presidents of some societies have special letters to signify their appointment. The president of the Royal Society has PRS after his name, for instance, but these letters are used only within the particular society.

The Companion of Literature (CLit) is an award bestowed by the Royal Society of Literature and limited to ten recipients. The letters CLit are placed before the fellowship: CLit, FRSL.

ROYAL ACADEMICIANS

It is not suggested that Royal Academicians yield in precedence to fellows of learned societies. In practice the two lists do not coincide. The president and past presidents are indicated as follows:

President of the Royal Academy	PRA
Past President of the Royal Academy	PPRA
President of the Royal Scottish Academy	PRSA
Past President of the Royal Scottish Academy	PPRSA

Royal Academicians and Associates are indicated as follows:

Royal Academician	RA
Royal Scottish Academician	RSA
Associate of the Royal Academy	ARA
Associate of the Royal Scottish Academy	ARSA

Similarly with other academies, such as president of the Royal Hibernian Academy (PRHA) and academicians (RHA).

Honorary academicians and associates do not normally use the relevant letters.

PROFESSIONAL BODIES

These letters are usually restricted to correspondence concerning the particular profession. As there is no recognised order for placing qualifications awarded by different bodies, a recipient usually places these letters on headed paper, business cards etc. in order of importance to his particular profession.

It is not suggested that professional societies as such yield precedence to learned societies, but the two groups do not coincide to any great extent. Most senior learned societies that elect fellows are senior in age and importance to the professional.

Those whose fellowships are by subscription are generally used only in the particular field of interest. For example, if Mr John Smith is a Chartered Engineer and a Fellow of the Royal Historical Society, he would normally be described professionally as John Smith, Esq, CEng, FIMechE. When corresponding on historical subjects, he is normally described as John Smith, Esq, FRHistS. If both series of letters are placed after his name, it is usual to place first those that concern the particular function or subject which is being addressed.

WRITERS TO THE SIGNET	It is customary for the letters WS to follow the name after university degrees and those that signify fellowship or membership of a society or institution, despite the fact that the WS Society, an ancient society of solicitors in Scotland, is considerably older than many institutions. This is a way of indicating the profession.
	It is not customary for the letters WS to be used socially.
MEMBERS OF PARLIAMENT	The letters MP are always shown for a Member of Parliament.
ROYAL NAVY	The letters RN, or the service's preferred 'Royal Navy', are placed after the names of serving officers of, and below, the rank of captain.
	They are also placed after the names of retired captains, commanders and lieutenant-commanders where they are prefixed by naval rank.
	The letters RNR are likewise used by officers of the Royal Naval Reserve.
ARMY	The appropriate letters that signify a regiment or corps may be placed after the name for officers on the active list of, and below, the rank of lieutenant-colonel, but are often omitted in social correspondence. These letters are not used for retired officers.
	Corps have letter abbreviations: for example, RE, RAMC, RAOC, RAPC. Most regiments are written in full.
ROYAL AIR FORCE	The letters RAF are placed after the names of serving and retired officers, except for Marshals of the Royal Air Force. Officers above the rank of Group Captain do not often use these letters.
	Similarly, the letters RAFVR are used for the Royal Air Force Volunteer Reserve.
ROYAL MARINES	The letters RM, or 'Royal Marines' in full, are placed after the names of serving and retired officers of and below the rank of lieutenant-colonel.
	Similarly, RMR for the Royal Marines Reserve.

Orders, Decorations

HONOURS	Victoria Cross	VC
CONFERRED BY	George Cross	GC
THE CROWN:	Knight of the Order of the Garter	KG
ORDER OF	Knight of the Thistle	KT
PRECEDENCE	Knight/Dame Grand Cross of the Order of the Bath	GCB
	Order of Merit	OM
	Knight Grand Commander of the Order of the Star of India	GCSI
	Knight/Dame Grand Cross of the Order of St Michael and St George	GCMG
	Knight Grand Commander of the Order of the Indian Empire	GCIE
	Knight/Dame Grand Cross of the Royal Victorian Order	GCVO
	Knight/Dame Grand Cross of the Order of the British Empire	GBE
	Companion of Honour	CH
	Knight Commander of the Order of the Bath	KCB
	Dame Commander of the Order of the Bath	DCB
	Knight Commander of the Order of the Star of India	KCSI
	Knight Commander of the Order of St Michael and St George	KCMG
	Dame Commander of the Order of St Michael and St George	DCMG
	Knight Commander of the Order of the Indian Empire	KCIE
	Knight Commander of the Royal Victorian Order	KCVO
	Dame Commander of the Royal Victorian Order	DCVO
	Knight Commander of the Order of the British Empire	KBE
	Dame Commander of the Order of the British Empire	DBE
	Companion of the Order of the Bath	CB
	Companion of the Order of the Star of India	CSI
	Companion of the Order of St Michael and St George	CMG
	Companion of the Order of the Indian Empire	CIE
	Commander of the Royal Victorian Order	CVO
	Commander of the Order of the British Empire	CBE
	Distinguished Service Order	DSO
	Lieutenant of the Royal Victorian Order	LVO
	Officer of the Order of the British Empire	OBE
	Imperial Service Order	ISO
	Member of the Royal Victorian Order	MVO
	Member of the Order of the British Empire	MBE
	Indian Order of Merit (Military)	IOM

Conspicuous Gallantry Cross	CGC
Royal Red Cross	RRC
Distinguished Service Cross	DSC
Military Cross	MC
Distinguished Flying Cross	DFC
Air Force Cross	AFC
Associate, Royal Red Cross	ARRC
Order of British India	OBI
Distinguished Conduct Medal	DCM
Conspicuous Gallantry Medal	CGM
George Medal	GM
Distinguished Conduct Medal of the Royal West African Frontier Force and the King's African Rifles	DCM
Indian Distinguished Service Medal	IDSM
Distinguished Service Medal	DSM
Military Medal	MM
Distinguished Flying Medal	DFM
Air Force Medal	AFM
Medal for Saving Life at Sea	SGM
Indian Order of Merit (Civil) *no longer bestowed*	IOM
Colonial Police Medal for Gallantry	CPM
Queen's Gallantry Medal	QGM
British Empire Medal *none since 1974*	BEM
King's Police Medal	KPM
King's Police and Fire Service Medal	KPFSM
Queen's Police Medal	QPM
Queen's Fire Service Medal	QFSM
Colonial Police Medal for Meritorious Service	CPM
Meritorious Service Medal	MSM
Army Emergency Reserve Decoration	ERD
Volunteer Officers' Decoration	VD
Territorial Decoration	TD
Efficiency Decoration	ED
Decoration for Officers of the Royal Naval Reserve	RD
Decoration for Officers of the Royal Naval Volunteer Reserve	VRD
Air Efficiency Award	AE
Canadian Forces Decoration	CD

ORDER OF LETTERS	The use of the letters of all honours that have been conferred by the Crown is obligatory, and should be placed after the name in order of precedence, for example John Brown, Esq, CBE, MVO, TD.
	The recipient is allowed to use the appropriate letters for the Order from the date of announcement in the *London Gazette*.
	A baronet has the letters Bt or Bart immediately after the name and before any letters which signify honours.
PROMOTION WITHIN ORDER	Those promoted within the same Order of Chivalry do not continue to show the letters of the lower class of that order. If Brigadier John Smith, OBE, is promoted to CBE, he is addressed as Brigadier John Smith, CBE, the OBE being dropped.
VC AND GC	It should be noted that VC and GC have precedence of all letters signifying Orders (including knightly grades therein), Decorations and Medals.
OM AND CH	The Order of Merit (OM) and Companion of Honour (CH) are important honours which bestow no title on the holder.
PC	Some people prefer PC after KG since that is its correct position in order of precedence.
COMMONWEALTH	Some Commonwealth countries have their own Orders, which are awarded to their citizens and indicated in the same way as the British system.
ORDER OF CANADA	The Order of Canada, of which the Queen is Sovereign, is divided into the following grades according to its last revised constitution:

CC   Companion of the Order of Canada with precedence after VC and GC before all other letters

OC   Officer of the Order of Canada, with precedence after CC

CM   Member of the Order of Canada, with precedence after OC

The Cross of Valour, the Star of Courage and the Medal of Bravery have no letters.

ORDER OF AUSTRALIA

The Order of Australia, of which the Queen is Sovereign, consists of a General Division and a Military Division and is divided into the following classes:

AK   Knight of the Order of Australia, with precedence after OM

AD   Dame of the Order of Australia, with the same precedence as AK

AC   Companion of the Order of Australia, with precedence after GBE

AO   Officer of the Order of Australia, with precedence after knight bachelor

AM   Member of the Order of Australia, with precedence after DSO

OAM   Medal of the Order of Australia, with precedence after RRC

ORDER OF NEW ZEALAND

The Order of New Zealand, of which the Queen is Sovereign, is a single first-level Order and consists of ordinary, additional and honorary members.

ONZ   Order of New Zealand, with precedence after VC and GC before all other letters

The Queen's Service Order of New Zealand is divided into two parts, for community service and for public service:

QSO   Companions of the Queen's Service Order, with precedence after OBE

QSM   The Queen's Service Medal, with precedence after QGM and before BEM

Styles by Office

Religion

The Church of England and the Anglican Communion

Women have been ordained into the Churches of England (1994), Scotland (1969), Wales (1996) and Ireland (1990), but cannot realise office above and including that of Bishop.

CHURCH OF ENGLAND AND ASSOCIATED CHURCHES IN THE ANGLICAN COMMUNITY

Ordained clergymen of the Church of England, and other churches within the Anglican Communion, do not receive the accolade of knighthood, though the letters signifying an order of knighthood are placed after the name: The Right Reverend the Lord Bishop of Brompton, KCVO.

Doctorate degrees should be added on the envelope where appropriate.

If a clergyman succeeds to a title or has a courtesy title or style, the ecclesiastical style precedes the temporal. For example: The Venerable Sir John Jones, Bt; The Reverend the Hon John Brown; The Very Reverend the Earl of Southend.

When it is desired to show that a clergyman has served in the Armed Forces – in a list of retired officers for example – the following form is used: The Reverend John Smith, Commander, Royal Navy.

'The Reverend' is often abbreviated to 'The Rev', although some clergymen prefer it to be written in full; others prefer the abbreviation 'The Revd'.

Spouses of the clergy do not have any special form of address.

Unless otherwise stated, deans, provosts, archdeacons, canons and prebendaries should be addressed formally in writing as 'Very Reverend Sir or Madam', and the letter concluded 'I have the honour to remain, Very Reverend Sir or Madam, your obedient servant' or 'Yours sincerely'.

THE ARCHBISHOPS OF CANTERBURY AND YORK

The Archbishops of Canterbury and York are privy counsellors and accordingly are addressed as 'The Most Reverend and Right Honourable...' and have seats in the House of Lords. The Archbishop of Canterbury is Primate of all England and Metropolitan. The Archbishop of York is Primate of England and Metropolitan.

ARCHBISHOPS OF THE CHURCH OF IRELAND & OTHER PROVINCES	There are two Archbishops of the Church of Ireland: 　Armagh (Primate of all Ireland) 　Dublin (Primate of Ireland)
RETIRED ARCHBISHOPS	Retired archbishops revert to the status of bishop. The former Archbishop of Canterbury is usually created a peer. The correct way to address retired archbishops is the same as that of retired bishops.
BISHOP OF LONDON	The Bishop of London is always a privy counsellor and accordingly is addressed as 'The Right Reverend and Right Honourable'.
BISHOPS, DIOCESAN AND SUFFRAGAN, CHURCH OF ENGLAND AND THE CHURCH IN WALES	The Bishops of London, Durham and Winchester have seats in the House of Lords. When a vacancy arises, it is filled by the senior diocesan bishop without a seat and the vacated See is placed at the foot of the list of those awaiting seats. Translation of a bishop from one See to another does not affect his right to sit in the House of Lords. The Bishop of Sodor and Man is an *ex officio* member of the Legislative Council of the Isle of Man. In each diocese of the Church of England, suffragan bishops are appointed on the recommendation of the bishop to assist him. These are styled by the name of some ancient town within the See. While enjoying full episcopal rights, they do not qualify for membership of the House of Lords. There has been controversy as to whether a suffragan bishop is entitled to the style of 'Lord' Bishop (that is, whether this title is ecclesiastical or temporal), but although the prefix is usually given by custom or courtesy, he is not so styled in an official document. The Church in Wales is a separate Province of the Anglican Communion; the office of Archbishop of Wales is held by one of their six diocesan bishops.
BISHOP, EPISCOPAL CHURCH IN SCOTLAND	Since the Episcopal Church is not the State Church of Scotland, a bishop has no official precedence and recognition and is, therefore, addressed as The Right Rev John Smith, Bishop of X, and not as The Right Rev the Bishop of X. Socially, the style is as for a diocesan bishop of the Church of England, except for the Primus of Scotland who acts as the Presiding Bishop. He is elected by the other bishops and has no Metropolitan power. The style is The Most Reverend the Primus.
BISHOPS, CHURCH OF IRELAND	Bishops are styled as diocesan bishops in the Church of England, except for the Bishop of Meath (Premier Bishop of the Church of Ireland) who is styled The Most Reverend instead of The Right Reverend.

DEAN	A dean is the incumbent of a cathedral or collegiate church, except when he or she is a provost.
PROVOST	A provost is usually an incumbent of a cathedral, which has been so created out of a parish church and whose responsibilities carry something in the nature of rector or vicar. Where a cathedral has a provost (not a dean), the freehold and the patronage is normally vested in the provost for the time being, and not in the chapter as would be normal were there a dean. In other respects duties are the same as a dean's.
ARCHDEACON	A senior clergyman whose duty it is to supervise the clergy and to administer part of a diocese, hence the territorial designation. As well as visitation duties, he or she is in charge of the fabric of parish churches and their contents.
RETIRED DEAN, PROVOST OR ARCHDEACON	The address is as for other clergy – that is, The Reverend in place of The Venerable – unless he or she remains a canon or prebendary, or is appointed to emeritus rank, when he or she is addressed accordingly. 'Emeritus' is used in official documents.
	A retired archdeacon is often incorrectly referred to as Archdeacon Smith but the word 'archdeacon' signifies an office not a rank. Strictly speaking, there cannot be an archdeacon emeritus though the title is often used.
CANON	A canon is either residentiary, with duties in a cathedral, or honorary. The latter is usually given to incumbents with a record of honourable service in the diocese. A minor canon is a cleric attached to a cathedral or collegiate church to assist in the daily services. The address is as for other clergy.
RETIRED CANON	The address is as for other clergy, unless appointed a canon emeritus, when he or she is addressed as previously. The word 'emeritus' is used only in official documents. Honorary canons usually retain their title unless they specifically resign it on leaving the diocese or retiring from the Church.
PREBENDARIES	Prebendaries have a Prebendal Stall in certain cathedrals or collegiate churches. The appointment is similar to a non-residentiary canon.
	After retirement, the address is as for other clergy, unless appointed a prebendary emeritus, when he or she is addressed as previously. The word 'emeritus' is used only in official documents.
RURAL DEAN	There is no special form of address, but he or she is often an honorary canon.

	SALUTATION	ENVELOPE	VERBAL ADDRESS	CONVERSATION
Archbishops of Canterbury and York	My Lord Archbishop or Your Grace (formal) Dear Lord Archbishop or Dear Archbishop (social)	The Most Reverend and Right Hon the Lord Archbishop of Canterbury/York	Your Grace (formal) Archbishop (social)	The Archbishop (of Canterbury/York)
Archbishops of the Church of Ireland and Other Provinces	My Lord Archbishop or Your Grace (formal) Dear Lord Archbishop or Dear Archbishop (social)	The Most Reverend the Lord Archbishop of Blank	Your Grace (formal) or Archbishop (social)	The Archbishop (of Blank)
Bishop of London	Dear Bishop	The Right Reverend and Right Hon the Lord Bishop of London	Bishop	The Bishop (of London)
Bishop, Diocesan and Suffragan, Church of England and the Church in Wales	Dear Bishop	The Right Reverend the Lord Bishop of Blank or The Right Reverend the Bishop of Blank	Bishop	The Bishop (of Blank)
Assistant and Retired Bishops	Dear Bishop	The Right Rev John Smith (if also a Privy Counsellor, The Right Rev and Right Hon John Smith)	Bishop	The Bishop (or by name, i.e. Bishop Smith)
Bishops, Episcopal Church in Scotland	Dear Primus	The Most Reverend the Primus	Primus	The Primus
Dean	Dear Dean	The Very Reverend the Dean of Norwich	Dean or Mr or Miss/Mrs/Ms Dean	The Dean (of Norwich)
Provost	Dear Provost	The Very Reverend the Provost of Coventry	Provost	The Provost (of Coventry)
Archdeacon	Dear Archdeacon	The Venerable the Archdeacon of Exeter	Archdeacon	The Archdeacon (of Exeter)

	SALUTATION	ENVELOPE	VERBAL ADDRESS	CONVERSATION
Canon	Dear Canon (Smith)	The Reverend Canon John Smith	Canon (Smith)	The Canon or Canon Smith
Prebendary	Dear Prebendary (Smith)	The Reverend Prebendary John Smith	Prebendary or Prebendary Smith	Prebendary or Prebendary Smith
Other Clergy	Dear Mr Smith , Dear Father Smith (For beneficed clergy Dear Rector or Dear Vicar)	The Reverend John Smith (Reverend Smith or The Reverend Smith is incorrect)	Mr Smith or Father Smith	Mr Smith or Father Smith (or Rector or The Vicar)

Chaplains to HM Forces

A chaplain serving with HM Forces is addressed in speech by ecclesiastical rank and never in speech by relative Service rank. It is not necessary to write the Service rank, but when used formally it must appear in brackets after the ecclesiastical title and before the chaplain's forename or initials.

The Chaplain of the Fleet, the Chaplain General to the Forces, Army, and the Chaplain-in-Chief, Royal Air Force, are archdeacons and therefore The Venerable is used. Letters begin with the appointment or name, 'Dear Chaplain General' or 'Dear Archdeacon Smith'. Envelopes are addressed accordingly – 'The Chaplain of the Fleet' or 'The Venerable John Smith' – followed by the appointment. Verbally, they are addressed by their appointment or as Archdeacon, as may be appropriate. The Deputy Chaplain General to the Forces, Army, the Principal Chaplain, Church of Scotland and Free Churches, Royal Navy or Royal Air Force and the Principal Roman Catholic Chaplain, Royal Navy, Army or Royal Air Force, are addressed by name or appointment. Principal Roman Catholic chaplains are Monsignori.

Other chaplains are addressed by name/appointment: for example, 'Dear Canon Jones', 'Dear Mr Jones' etc. If the name is used, the appointment is placed after the name, for example: The Reverend John Jones, OBE, MA, CF, Assistant Chaplain General, HQ, Blankshire Command. The letters RN or RAF are placed after the names of chaplains to these Services, following any decorations etc. Army chaplains have the letters CF after the name, following any decorations etc. Verbally a chaplain is addressed by name, by appointment or by ecclesiastical title or, informally, as Padre.

When the chaplain's name is not known, correspondence should be addressed to, for example, The Church of England Chaplain, RAF Station, Blanktown. Correspondence to a Jewish chaplain is addressed to, for example, The Reverend David Smith, CF, Senior Jewish Chaplain, Blanktown Garrison, etc; the verbal address is Rabbi, Minister or Padre, as may be appropriate.

Church of Scotland

This is the Established Church in Scotland, and is Presbyterian by constitution. The Supreme Court of the Church is the General Assembly that meets annually in May and is presided over by a Moderator, who is appointed each year by the Assembly.

The Sovereign either attends in person or is represented by the Lord High Commissioner to the General Assembly, who is appointed by the Crown.

LORD HIGH COMMISSIONER TO THE GENERAL ASSEMBLY

The same style is used for men and women. A letter begins 'Your Grace' and ends 'I have the honour to remain, Your Grace's most devoted and obedient servant'. The envelope is addressed to 'His or Her Grace the Lord High Commissioner'.

The verbal address is 'Your Grace', while the description in conversation is 'The Lord High Commissioner'.

MODERATOR OF THE GENERAL ASSEMBLY

A formal letter begins 'Dear Sir or Madam' or 'Dear Moderator' or, socially, as 'Dear Mr Smith' or 'Dear Moderator'. The envelope is addressed to 'The Rt Rev the Moderator of the General Assembly of the Church of Scotland' or 'The Rt Rev John Smith'.

The verbal address is 'Moderator' or, in conversation, 'The Moderator'.

FORMER MODERATOR

After his year of office, a former moderator is styled The Very Reverend John Smith; otherwise as Mr Smith or Mr Minister.

DEAN OF THE CHAPEL ROYAL AND DEAN OF THE THISTLE

They are styled The Very Reverend.

One person can hold both appointments.

OTHER CLERGY

Other clergy are addressed at the beginning of a formal letter as 'Dear Sir' or 'Dear Minister' or, socially, as 'Dear Mr or Miss/Mrs/Ms Smith or Dear Minister'.

The envelope would be addressed to 'The Reverend John Smith', followed by 'The Minister of Blanktown' (if Minister of a Parish). If a lady were ordained, she would be styled 'The Reverend Mary Smith'. Miss/Mrs/Ms should not be used.

Verbally, they are addressed as 'Mr Smith' or 'Minister'. In conversation, they are described as 'Mr Smith' or 'The Minister'.

Roman Catholic Church

The territorial designation and the term 'My Lord' are not officially recognised within the United Kingdom and, accordingly, are not used in official communications and documents. Hence, in these communications archbishops, bishops, abbots and priors are addressed by name and not by their province, dioceses, etc.

CARDINAL If a cardinal is appointed to a See, the address may be by appointment: for example, His Eminence Cardinal Smith. The territorial designation is not officially used when letters are addressed to the person and not to the province or diocese.

ARCHBISHOP On retirement, a Roman Catholic archbishop is appointed to a titular See and is then normally addressed by name.

BISHOP Roman Catholic bishops are styled Right Reverend, except in Ireland where they are styled Most Reverend. In Ireland, the abbreviation 'Dr' is included on the envelope before the name, as in 'The Most Reverend Dr John Smith, Bishop of Kildare'.

In lists by non-Roman Catholic organisations, a Roman Catholic bishop should be mentioned by name, for example: The Right Reverend Bishop Brown. If the territorial designation is given, and there is an Anglican Bishop whose See has the same name, it should be stated, as in 'Roman Catholic Bishop of Lancaster'.

Letter endings to bishops now tend to be more informal than they were in the past.

On retirement from his See or office, a bishop is appointed to a titular See, and addressed by name. Though it is not the usual practice, the titular See may be appended on the envelope after the name if desired.

MONSIGNOR Monsignor is a title held by virtue of a particular office, a Protonotary Apostolic, a Prelate of Honour or a Chaplain to his Holiness the Pope.

Monsignori are addressed as The Reverend instead of The Right Reverend or The Very Reverend.

PROVINCIAL The Provincial is the Superior of a Province in a Religious Order, such as the Dominicans, the Franciscans or the Jesuits.

LAY BROTHERS They are verbally addressed as Brother and referred to as Brother John.

	SALUTATION	SIGN OFF	ENVELOPE	VERBAL ADDRESS & CONVERSATION
The Pope	Your Holiness or Most Holy Father	For Roman Catholics: I have the honour to be, Your Holiness's most devoted and obedient child (or most humble child or, for non-Roman Catholics, obedient servant)	His Holiness the Pope	Verbal: Your Holiness Conversation: His Holiness or The Pope
Cardinal	Your Eminence or My Lord Cardinal (formal) or Dear Cardinal Smith (social)	I have the honour to be, My Lord Cardinal, Your Eminence's devoted and obedient child (very formal) or I remain, Your Eminence, Yours faithfully (formal) or I have the honour to be Your Eminence's obedient servant (officially recognised) or Yours Sincerely (social)	His Eminence the Cardinal Archbishop of Westminster (if an archbishop) or His Eminence Cardinal Smith (if not an archbishop)	Verbal: Your Eminence (formal) or Cardinal (Smith) (social) Conversation: His Eminence (formal) or Cardinal (Smith) (social)
Archbishop	My Lord Archbishop (formal) or Most Reverend Sir or Dear Archbishop (social)	I have the honour to be, Your Grace's devoted and obedient child (very formal) or I remain, Your Grace, Yours faithfully (formal), or I have the honour to be, Most Reverend Sir, Your obedient servant (officially recognised) or Yours sincerely (social)	His Grace the Archbishop of Sydney or The Most Reverend Archbishop Smith	Verbal: Your Grace (formal) or Archbishop (social) Conversation: His Grace (formal) or Archbishop (of Blank) (social)
Bishop	My Lord or My Lord Bishop (formal), Right Reverend Sir (officially recognised) or Dear Bishop (Smith) (social)	I have the honour to be, Your Lordship's obedient child (very formal), I remain, My Lord, Yours faithfully (formal) or I have the honour to be, Right Reverend Sir, Your obedient servant (or Most Reverend Sir for an Irish bishop) (officially recognised) or Yours sincerely (social)	His Lordship the Bishop of Blank or The Right Reverend John Smith, Bishop of Blank or The Right Reverend John Smith Auxiliary Bishop of Blank (formal and social) or The Right Reverend Bishop Smith (officially recognised)	Verbal: My Lord or My Lord Bishop Conversation: His Lordship or The Bishop

	SALUTATION	SIGN OFF	ENVELOPE	VERBAL ADDRESS & CONVERSATION
Abbot	My Lord Abbot or Right Reverend and Dear Father Abbot (formal), Right Reverend Sir (officially recognised) or Dear Father Abbot (social)	I beg to remain, My Lord Abbot, Your devoted and obedient servant (very formal for Roman Catholics) or Yours faithfully (formal) or Yours sincerely (social)	The Right Reverend the Abbot of Blank (followed by initials of his order) (formal and social) or The Right Reverend John Smith (initials of order) (officially recognised)	Verbal: The Abbot (of Blank) Conversation: Father Abbot (formal) or Abbot (social)
Monsignor	Reverend Sir (formal) or Dear Monsignor Smith or Dear Monsignor (social)		The Reverend Monsignor John Smith or The Reverend Monsignor or The Very Reverend Monsignor (Canon) John Smith (if he is a Canon)	Verbal: Monsignor or Monsignor Smith Conversation: Monsignor Smith
Provincial	Very Reverend Father Provincial or Very Reverend Father (formal) or Dear Father Provincial or Dear Father Smith (social)		Very Reverend Father Provincial (initials of order) or Very Reverend Father or The Very Reverend Father Smith (initials of order)	Father Provincial
Prior	Very Reverend (very formal) or Dear Father Prior (formal and social)		The Very Reverend the Prior of Blank or The Very Reverend John Smith (initials of order)	Verbal: Father Prior Conversation: The Prior (of Blank)
Canon	Very Reverend Sir (formal) or Dear Canon (Smith) (social)		The Very Reverend Canon John Smith	Canon Smith
Priest	Dear Reverend Father (formal) or Dear Father Smith (social)		The Reverend John Smith or The Reverend Fr Smith	Verbal: Father Conversation: Father Smith

Methodist Church & Other Leading Denominations

MINISTERS The beginning of a letter is Dear Sir/Madam (formal), or Dear Mr or Miss/Mrs/Ms Smith (social) and the envelope The Reverend John Smith. Miss/Mrs/Ms should not be used.

The verbal address is Mr or Miss/Mrs/Ms Smith and in conversation referred to as The Minister, The Pastor, The President or Dr/Mr/Miss/Mrs/Ms Smith.

DEACONESS OF THE METHODIST CHURCH She is referred to as Sister Jane Smith and is known in her community as Sister Jane. In a writing she may be referred to as Deaconess Jane Smith.

Islam

There is no central organisation or authority for Islam.

For further information, contact: Muslim Council of Great Britain
Boardman House, 64 Broadway, Stratford, London E15 1NT
Tel: 020 8432 0585/6
Website: www.mcb.org.uk

The Jewish Religion

The Chief Rabbi is styled as Chief Rabbi of the United Hebrew Congregation of the British Commonwealth of Nations. The Chief Rabbi Emeritus is styled as for the Chief Rabbi, with the addition of 'Emeritus'. A rabbi who holds a doctorate uses that style of address; the envelope would read 'Rabbi Dr …'.

	SALUTATION	ENVELOPE	VERBAL ADDRESS	CONVERSATION
Chief Rabbi	Dear Sir (formal) or Dear Chief Rabbi (social)	The Chief Rabbi Dr John Winkleman	Chief Rabbi	The Chief Rabbi
Rabbi	Dear Sir or Madam (formal) or Dear Rabbi Winkleman (social)	Rabbi J Winkleman	Rabbi Winkleman	Rabbi Winkleman
Ministers	Dear Sir or Reverend Sir (formal) or Dear Mr Winkleman (social)	The Reverend John Winkleman	Mr Winkleman	Mr Winkleman

Academics

Chancellors, vice-chancellors etc. are addressed according to rank and name, but can be addressed by office if the subject is pertaining to the university.

VICE-CHANCELLOR: CAMBRIDGE AND OXFORD
The formal title for the Vice-Chancellor of Cambridge is 'The Right Worshipful the Vice-Chancellor of the University of Cambridge'. The Vice-Chancellor of Oxford is 'The Reverend the Vice-Chancellor of the University of Oxford', irrespective of whether he/she is in Holy Orders. This is now only used for formal occasions.

HEAD OF COLLEGE
The title of the head of college varies from college to college. If the head of a college is also in Holy Orders, the ecclesiastical rank precedes the name or appointment.

PROFESSOR
A professor is addressed by name. On retirement, if emeritus rank is conferred, the professor emeritus/emeritus professor is addressed as previously in correspondence.

DOCTORATES
The recipient of a doctorate (or honorary doctorate) conferred by a university or other awarding body is entitled to be addressed as Doctor.

ORDER OF PLACING LETTERS OF DEGREES AFTER THE NAME
The order of placing the appropriate letters after the name depends upon the precedence of faculties within the conferring university, and whether a particular university places the degrees conferred in descending order (in order of seniority) or in ascending order (the order by which they are taken). Most universities adopt the 'ascending order' system. The position of the appropriate letters vary according to the awarding university and the name of the degree or the letters to indicate it:

Doctor of Civil Law	Oxford	DCL
Doctor of Law	Cambridge	LLD
Doctor of Laws	Other universities	LLD
Doctor of Letters	Cambridge, Leeds, Liverpool, Manchester and Sheffield	LittD
Doctor of Letters	Oxford and other universities	DLitt
Doctor of Literature	London and Belfast	DLit
Doctor of Music	Cambridge and Manchester	MusD
Doctor of Music	Oxford and other universities	DMus
Doctor of Philosophy	Oxford, Sussex, Ulster and York	DPhil
Doctor of Philosophy	Other universities	PhD

	SALUTATION	ENVELOPE	VERBAL ADDRESS	CONVERSATION
Chancellor (formal)	Dear Chancellor	The Chancellor of the University of X	Chancellor (on a platform) otherwise according to rank and name	The Chancellor or by name
Chancellor (social)	by name	Sir John Jones, KBE, Chancellor of the University of X	by name, or Chancellor	The Chancellor or by name
High Steward – if the subject concerns his or her university (formal)	Dear High Steward	The High Steward of the University of Oxford or The Rt Hon the Viscount Blank, The High Steward of the University of Oxford		
High Steward – if the subject concerns his or her university (social)	Dear High Steward	The High Steward of the University of Oxford or Viscount Blank, The High Steward of the University of Oxford		
Vice-Chancellor (formal)	Dear Sir or Madam or Dear Vice-Chancellor or Dear Mr Vice-Chancellor (Oxford)	The Vice-Chancellor, The University of X	Vice-Chancellor (on a platform) or by name	The Vice-Chancellor or by name
Vice-Chancellor (social)	By name or Dear Vice-Chancellor	Sir John Jones, KBE, Vice-Chancellor, University of X	Vice-Chancellor (on a platform) or by name	The Vice-Chancellor or by name
Professor (formal)	Dear Sir or Madam	Professor John Smith	Professor Smith	Professor Smith
Professor (social)	Dear Professor Jones	Professor Sue Jones	Professor Jones	Professor Jones
Doctor (formal)	Dear Sir or Madam	Dr John Smith	Dr Smith	Dr Smith
Doctor (social)	Dear Dr Jones	Dr Sue Jones	Dr Jones	Dr Jones

The Armed Forces

Relative Ranks

ROYAL NAVY	ARMY	ROYAL AIR FORCE
Admiral of the Fleet	Field Marshal	Marshal of the Royal Air Force
Admiral	General	Air Chief Marshal
Vice Admiral	Lieutenant-General	Air Marshal
Rear Admiral	Major-General	Air Vice-Marshal
Commodore	Brigadier	Air Commodore

Officers of the same rank show seniority according to length of service.

Officers with a title, or a courtesy title or style, are addressed in the same way as others with the same style. Some, however, prefer to be addressed by their service rank.

The Royal Navy

THE SENIOR SERVICE
As the Senior Service, naval officers should be considered senior to their equivalent ranks in the other services.

'RN' AFTER NAME
All officers below the rank of rear admiral are entitled to the words Royal Navy or the letters RN after their name. This is preceded by any decorations.

ADDRESS BY RANK ONLY
In informal correspondence certain officers are addressed by their rank only: commodore, rear admiral, vice admiral and Admiral of the Fleet (shortened to Admiral).

RETIRED OFFICERS
The rank of Admiral of the Fleet is held for life. Other officers of the rank of lieutenant-commander and above customarily use, and are addressed by, their rank after being placed on the retired list. The word 'retired' (abbreviated to 'Ret' or 'Rtd') should not be added after an officer's name in ordinary correspondence or lists, but only when it is necessary to indicate that an officer is on the retired list.

MEDICAL OFFICERS	The ranks of naval medical officers are preceded by 'Surgeon': for example, Surgeon Rear Admiral Sir John Green, KBE.		
DENTAL OFFICERS	The ranks of naval dental officers are preceded by 'Surgeon' and suffixed '(D)': for example, Surgeon Lieutenant (D) Judith Green, RN.		
NAVAL INSTRUCTOR OFFICERS	The ranks of naval instructor officers are preceded by 'Instructor': for example Instructor Commander James Smith, Royal Navy.		
ROYAL NAVAL RESERVE	Forms of address are as for the Royal Navy except for Royal Naval Reserve (or RNR) after the name.		
ROYAL MARINES	Forms of address are as for the Army. Those of the rank of lieutenant-colonel and below place RM (or Royal Marines in full) after their name.		
VERBAL ADDRESS	A more junior officer would address a superior as 'Sir' or 'Ma'am'.		

	SALUTATION	ENVELOPE	VERBAL ADDRESS	CONVERSATION
Admiral of the Fleet	According to title or Dear Admiral Brown	Admiral of the Fleet Sir John Brown, GBE, KCG	According to title or Admiral	According to title. If reference is made to rank, Admiral of the Fleet is used in full
Admiral	According to title or Dear Admiral Edwards	Admiral Sir George Edwards, KBE	According to title or Admiral Edwards	According to title or Admiral Edwards
Vice Admiral	According to title or Dear Admiral Williams		According to title or Admiral Williams	According to title or Admiral Williams
Rear Admiral	According to title or Dear Admiral Hayes		According to title or Admiral Hayes	According to title or Admiral Hayes
Commodore or Captain	Dear Commodore Evans Dear Captain Evans	Commodore John Evans, CBE, Royal Navy Captain Jane Evans, CB, Royal Navy	Commodore Evans Captain Evans	Commodore Evans Captain Evans
Commander or Lieutenant-Commander	Dear Commander Mills Dear Lieutenant-Commander Mills	Commander Henry Mills, OBE, Royal Navy Lieutenant-Commander Henry Mills, Royal Navy	Commander Mills	Commander Mills

The Army

RETIRED OFFICERS

The rank of field marshal is held for life. Other regular officers of the rank of Major and above may use, and be addressed by, their rank after being placed on the retired list.

The word 'retired' (abbreviated to 'Ret' or 'Rtd') should not be added after an officer's name in ordinary correspondence or in lists, but only when it is specifically necessary to indicate that an officer is on the retired list.

ADDRESS BY RANK

NCOs are addressed according to their rank. A lance corporal is called 'Corporal'. These ranks may be used with or without the surname.

A more junior officer would address a superior as 'Sir' or 'Ma'am'.

THE HOUSEHOLD DIVISION

This comprises the Household Cavalry and The Guards' Division.

The principal ranks of the Household Cavalry (The Life Guards, and The Blues and Royals) are as follows:

Warrant Officer Class I, Regimental Corporal Major (RCM)
Warrant Officer Class II, Squadron Corporal Major (SCM)
Staff Corporal (SCpl)
Corporal of Horse (CoH)
Corporal (Cpl)
Lance Corporal (LCpl)
Trooper (Tpr)

The principal ranks of the Guards' Division (formerly The Brigade of Guards) are:

Warrant Officer Class I (RSM)
Warrant Officer Class II (CSM, etc.)
Colour Sergeant (CSgt) and Company Quartermaster Sergeant (CQMS)
Sergeant (Sgt)
Lance Sergeant (LSgt)
Lance Corporal (LCpl)
Guardsman (Gdsm)

	SALUTATION	ENVELOPE	VERBAL ADDRESS	CONVERSATION
Field Marshal	According to title	Field Marshal the Lord Brown, GCB	According to title	According to title. If reference is made to rank, Field Marshal Brown or Field Marshal is used in full
General	According to title or Dear General Jones	General Sir Edward Jones, KBE	According to title or General Jones	According to title or General Jones
Lieutenant-General	According to title or Dear General Jones	Lieutenant-General George Jones	According to title or General Jones	According to title or General Jones
Major-General	According to title or Dear General Smith	Major-General Edward Smith, CBE	According to title or General Smith	According to title or General Smith
Brigadier	Dear Brigadier French	Brigadier Charles French	Brigadier French or Brigadier	Brigadier French

		SALUTATION	ENVELOPE	VERBAL ADDRESS
HOUSEHOLD CAVALRY	Regimental Corporal Major	Dear Mr Smith	According to rank, which may be abbreviated, as in RCM	Mr Smith
	Squadron Corporal Major	Dear Corporal Major Jones	As above	Corporal Major Jones
	Corporal of Horse	Dear Corporal Evans	As above	Corporal Evans
THE GUARDS' DIVISION	Regimental Sergeant Major	Dear Sergeant Major Brown	According to rank, which may be abbreviated, as in RSM.	Sergeant Major Brown
	Other warrant officers	By rank and name	As above	By rank and name

The Royal Air Force

All officers below the rank of Marshal of the Royal Air Force are entitled to the letters RAF after their name. This is preceded by any decorations.

ROYAL AIR FORCE VOLUNTEER RESERVE

Officers should only use, and be addressed by, their ranks when under training or when called up for service.

Forms of address are then as for the Royal Air Force except that the letters RAFVR follow the name (in lieu of RAF)

RETIRED OFFICERS

The rank of Marshal of the Royal Air Force is held for life. Other officers of the rank of flight-lieutenant and above may use, and be addressed by, their rank after being placed on the retired list.

The word 'retired' (or the abbreviation 'Ret' or 'Rtd') need not be added after an officer's name, but officially it has been the practice for the Ministry of Defence to use the abbreviation 'Retd' for officers on the retired list.

VERBAL ADDRESS

A more junior officer would address a superior as 'Sir' or 'Ma'am'.

	SALUTATION	ENVELOPE	VERBAL ADDRESS	CONVERSATION
Marshal of the Royal Air Force	According to title or, if rank is preferred, Dear Air Marshal Jenkins	Marshal of the Royal Air Force Viscount Peckham, GCB	According to title	According to title
Air Chief Marshal	According to title or Dear Air Marshal Smith	Air Chief Marshal Sir John Smith, KBE	According to title or Air Marshal Smith	According to title or Air Marshal Smith
Air Marshal	According to title or Dear Air Marshal Smith	Air Chief Marshal Sir John Smith, KBE	According to title or Air Marshal Smith	According to title or Air Marshal Smith
Air Vice Marshal	According to title or Dear Air Marshal Smith	Air Chief Marshal Sir John Smith, KBE	According to title or Air Marshal Smith	According to title or Air Marshal Smith
Air Commodore	According to title or Dear Air Commodore Smith	Air Commodore John Smith	Air Commodore Smith	Air Commodore Smith

Diplomatic Service

Ambassadors accredited to the Court of St James's are styled His (or Her) Excellency. High Commissioners are accorded the same style and precedence as ambassadors.

British ambassadors are known as His (or Her) Excellency within the country to which they are accredited but not in the United Kingdom. Governors-General and Governors are also styled His (or Her) Excellency.

The formal style is now viewed as old-fashioned. It is acceptable to use the social style in almost all instances. A lady Ambassador is called Ambassador, and not Ambassadress.

	SALUTATION	VALEDICTION	ENVELOPE	VERBAL ADDRESS	CONVERSATION
Ambassador (formal)	Your Excellency	I have the honour to be, with the highest consideration, Your Excellency's obedient servant	His Excellency, The Ambassador of Denmark or His Excellency Mr Nils Jensen	Your Excellency should be mentioned at least once in conversation, and thereafter Sir or Ma'am or by name	His Excellency
Ambassador (social)	Dear Ambassador	Yours sincerely	His Excellency, The Ambassador of Denmark or His Excellency Mr Nils Jensen	Ambassador or by name	The Danish Ambassador or The Ambassador of Denmark or by name
High Commissioner (formal)	Your Excellency	I have the honour to be Your Excellency's obedient servant	Her Excellency, The High Commissioner of South Africa or Her Excellency Miss Grace Mpahlele	Your Excellency should be mentioned at least once in conversation, and thereafter Sir or Ma'am or by name	His Excellency
High Commissioner (social)	Dear High Commissioner	Yours sincerely	Her Excellency, The High Commissioner of South Africa or Her Excellency Miss Grace Mpahlele	High Commissioner or by name	The South African High Commissioner or The High Commissioner of South Africa or by name

Law

England and Wales

The Lord High Chancellor, colloquially the Lord Chancellor, receives a peerage on appointment. The chief judicial officer in England, he vacates office with the government.

The Lord Chief Justice of England is a privy counsellor and, on appointment, is raised to the peerage.

The Master of the Rolls and the President of the Family Division are knighted on appointment and are members of the Privy Council; they are addressed according to judicial rank. Lords of Appeal in Ordinary are members of the Privy Council and are created peers.

A Lord Justice of the Court of Appeal will normally have been created a knight or dame as a judge of the High Court of Justice and will also be a member of the Privy Council.

Judges of the High Court of Justice are knighted on appointment, or made Dame of the Most Excellent Order of the British Empire, and will also be a member of the Privy Council.

High Court judges retire when they are 75. On retirement, the prefix The Honourable and the style The Hon Mr/Mrs Justice are dropped.

If a Queen's Counsel when at the Bar, circuit judges retain the letters QC after the name. On retirement circuit judges lose the style 'Judge', becoming His Hon John Smith.

The forename is used if there is more than one judge with the same surname.

Scotland

A Senator (judge) of the College of Justice is known as a Lord of Session. On taking his seat on the Bench he is given a judicial title by which he is known both in office and on retirement.

The Lord Justice General and the Lord Justice Clerk are addressed by their appointments and not their judicial titles. The Lord Justice General is invariably a privy counsellor.

The chairman of a Scottish Land Court receives a judicial title on appointment. He is thus styled as a Lord of Session.

ENGLAND & WALES	SALUTATION	ENVELOPE	VERBAL ADDRESS	CONVERSATION
Lord Chancellor	My Lord (formal) or Dear Lord Chancellor (social)	The Rt Hon the Lord Chancellor	According to title or Lord Chancellor	According to title or The Lord Chancellor
Lord Chief Justice	My Lord (formal) or Dear Lord Chief Justice (social)	The Rt Hon the Lord Chief Justice of England	According to title or Lord Chief Justice	According to title or The Lord Chief Justice
Master of the Rolls	Dear Master of the Rolls or Dear Sir John	The Rt Hon the Master of the Rolls	According to title or Master of the Rolls	According to title or The Master of the Rolls
President of the Family Division	Dear President or Dear Dame Margaret	The Rt Hon the President of the Family Division	According to title or President	According to title or The President of the Family Division
Lord of Appeal in Ordinary	Dear Lord Roch	The Lord Roch, PC	According to title	According to title
Lord Justice of the Court of Appeal	Dear Lord Justice	The Rt Hon the Lord Justice Smith	Lord Justice	The Lord Justice or His Lordship (judicial matters)
Judge of the High Court (Male)	Sir or My Lord or Dear Judge	The Hon Mr Justice Smith or Sir John Smith	My Lord or Mr Justice Smith or Sir John	
Judge of the High Court (female)	Madam or Dear Dame Elizabeth	The Hon Mrs Justice Lane or The Hon Dame Elizabeth Lane	My Lady or Mrs Justice Lane or Dame Elizabeth (Lane)	
Circuit Judge	Dear Judge	His Hon Judge Wells	Judge or according to title	

SCOTLAND	SALUTATION	ENVELOPE	VERBAL ADDRESS	CONVERSATION
Lord of Session	My Lord (formal) or according to judicial title (e.g. Lord Smith)	The Hon Lord Cameron or The Rt Hon Lord Smith (if a privy counsellor)	My Lord or Lord Smith	Lord Smith
Lord Justice General	My Lord (formal) or Dear Lord Justice General	The Rt Hon the Lord Chief Justice of England	My Lord or Lord Justice General	Lord Justice General
Lord Justice Clerk	My Lord (formal) or Dear Lord Justice Clerk	The Hon the Lord Justice Clerk or The Rt Hon the Lord Justice Clerk (if a privy counsellor)	My Lord or Lord Justice Clerk	Lord Justice Clerk

Medicine

There are distinct forms of address for medicine and surgery.

	SALUTATION	ENVELOPE	VERBAL ADDRESS	CONVERSATION
DOCTOR	Dear Dr Faulks	Dr Petra Faulks, MD,FRCP	Dr Faulks	Dr Faulks
PHYSICIAN	Dear Dr Jones	Dr Helen Jones, MB,BS	Dr Jones	Dr Jones
SURGEON	Dear Mr Forde	William Forde, Esq, MS,FRCS	Mr Forde	Mr Forde

Letters after the name denoting medical qualifications follow any Crown honours and are placed in the following order: doctorates, mastership, baccalaureates, postgraduate diplomas (fellowships/memberships except MRCS), qualifying diplomas (MRCS, LRCP etc.).

DOCTORATES *Doctor of...*	DM, MD	Medicine
	DCh	Surgery
	DChD	Dental Surgery
MASTERSHIPS *Master of...*	MC, MCh, MChir, MS, CM, ChM	Surgery
	MDS	Dental Surgery
	MAO	Art of Obstetrics
	MCB	Clinical Biochemistry
	MChOrth	Orthopaedic Surgery
	MCHOtol	Otology
	MClinPsychol	Clinical Psychology
	MCommH	Community Health
BACCALAUREATES *Bachelor of...*	BM, MB	Medicine
	BCh, BChir, BS, ChB	Surgery
	BDS	Dental Surgery
	BAO	Art of Obstetrics
	BAc	Acupuncture
	BASc	Applied Science
	BDSc	Dental Science
	BHy, BHyg	Hygiene
	BPharm	Pharmacy

POSTGRADUATE DIPLOMAS: FELLOWSHIPS *Fellow of the Royal College of...*

FRCP	Physicians
FRCPEd	Physicians of Edinburgh
FRCPI	Physicians of Ireland
FRCP (Glas)	Physicians and Surgeons of Glasgow (physician)
FRCS	Surgeons
FRCSEd	Surgeons of Edinburgh
FRCSI	Surgeons of Ireland
FRCS(Glas)	Physicians and Surgeons of Glasgow (surgeon)
FRCOG	Obstetricians and Gynaecologists
FRCGP	General Practitioners
FRCPath	Pathologists
FRCPsych	Psychiatrists
FRCR	Radiologists

POSTGRADUATE DIPLOMAS: *Member of the Royal College of...*

MRCP	Physicians
MRCPEd	Physicians of Edinburgh
MRCPI	Physicians of Ireland
MRCP(Glas)	Physicians and Surgeons of Glasgow
MRCP(UK)	Physicians and Surgeons of the United Kingdom
MRCOG	Obstetricians and Gynaecologists
MRCGP	General Practitioners
MRCPath	Pathologists
MRCPsych	Psychiatrists
FFA RCS	Fellow of the Faculty of Anaesthetists, Royal College of Surgeons
FDS RCS	Fellow in Dental Surgery, Royal College of Surgeons
FFCM	Fellow of the Faculty of Community Medicine
MFCM	Member of the Faculty of Community Medicine

POSTGRADUATE DIPLOMAS: QUALIFYING DIPLOMAS

MRCS	Member of the Royal College of Surgeons
LRCP	Licentiate of the Royal College of Physicians
LRCS	Licentiate of the Royal College of Surgeons of Edinburgh
LRFPS	Licentiate of the Royal Faculty of Physicians and Surgeons of Glasgow
LRCPS	Licentiate of the Royal College of Physicians and Surgeons of Glasgow
LRCPI	Licentiate of the Royal College of Physicians of Ireland
LRCSI	Licentiate of the Royal College of Surgeons of Ireland
LM	Licentiate in Midwifery
LSA	Licentiate of the Society of Apothecaries
LMSSA	Licentiate in Medicine and Surgery, Society of Apothecaries

Police

There is no longer any differentiation between male and female officers. CID officers add the prefix 'detective' in the ranks from constable to chief superintendent.

At the beginning of a letter to a chief inspector, inspector, police sergeant or police constable, the appropriate rank is placed before the name, e.g. Dear Chief Inspector Smith. The rank is placed on the envelope before the name. Police sergeant is often abbreviated to PS, police constable to PC, detective sergeant to DS and detective constable to DC.

The following does not differ in Scotland and Northern Ireland.

	SALUTATION	ENVELOPE	VERBAL ADDRESS	CONVERSATION
Commissioner (Metropolitan Police)	According to title or Dear Commissioner	Sir Charles Maxwell, KBE, Commissioner of Police for the Metropolis	According to title or Commissioner	According to title or The Commissioner
Commissioner (City of London Police)	According to title or Dear Commissioner	Sir Charles Maxwell, KBE, Commissioner of Police for the City of London	According to title or Commissioner	According to title or The Commissioner
Chief Constable (other Police Forces)	According to title or Dear Chief Constable	Sir John Smith, KBE, Chief Constable, Gloucestershire Constabulary	According to title or Commissioner	According to title or The Commissioner
Deputy Commissioner (Metropolitan Police)	According to title or Dear Deputy Commissioner	John Smith, Esq, Deputy Commissioner of Police for the City of London	According to title or Deputy Commissioner	According to title or The Deputy Commissioner
Assistant Commissioner (Metropolitan Police)	According to title or Dear Assistant Commissioner	John Smith, Esq, Assistant Commissioner of Police for the City of London	According to title or Assistant Commissioner	According to title or The Assistant Commissioner
Commander	According to title or Dear Commander Jones	Commander G H Jones, Metropolitan Police	According to title or Commander	According to title or The Commander

Politics

All Cabinet Ministers of the United Kingdom Parliament are also members of the Privy Council. They accordingly have the prefix 'The Rt Hon' before their names; this also takes the place of Mrs/Miss/Ms before a woman's name.

All members of the House of Commons have the letters MP after their name.

There is no special form of address for the partner of either a privy counsellor or a Member of Parliament.

If the writer knows the minister concerned, and the letter broadly relates to his or her department, it is permissible to write to him/her by appointment, e.g. Dear Prime Minister or Dear Lord Chancellor etc.

	SALUTATION	ENVELOPE	VERBAL ADDRESS	CONVERSATION
Prime Minister	Dear Prime Minister	The Rt Hon Margaret Chamberlain, MP the Prime Minister	Prime Minister	The Prime Minister
Deputy Prime Minister	Dear Deputy Prime Minister	The Rt Hon Thomas Keenan, MP, the Deputy Prime Minister	Deputy Prime Minister	The Deputy Prime Minister
Chancellor of the Exchequer	Dear Chancellor	The Rt Hon Charles Finnigan, MP, the Chancellor of the Exchequer	Chancellor of the Exchequer	The Chancellor of the Exchequer
Lord Privy Seal	Dear Lord Privy Seal	The Rt Hon the Lord Ansson, PC, the Lord Privy Seal	Lord Privy Seal	The Lord Privy Seal
President of the Board of Trade	Dear President	The Rt Hon the President of the Board of Trade	President	The President of the Board of Trade
Minister	Dear Minister or by name	The Rt Hon Anthony Gordon, MP, Secretary of State for the Environment	Minister	The Secretary of State for the Environment or by name
Backbencher	Dear Mr Williams	Richard Williams Esq, MP	Mr Williams	Mr Williams

Local Government

A Lord-Lieutenant is the Sovereign's representative in each county. In Scotland, the Lord Provosts of the cities of Aberdeen, Dundee, Edinburgh and Glasgow are *ex officio* Lord-Lieutenants for their respective cities. The Crown appoints a Lord-Lieutenant for each of the following regions:

ENGLAND

Bedfordshire	Lancashire
Berkshire	Leicestershire
Bristol	Lincolnshire
Buckinghamshire	Merseyside
Cambridgeshire	Norfolk
Cheshire	Northamptonshire
Cornwall	Northumberland
Cumbria	North Yorkshire
Derbyshire	Nottinghamshire
Devon	Oxfordshire
Dorset	Rutland
Durham	Shropshire
East Riding of Yorkshire	Somerset
East Sussex	South Yorkshire
Essex	Staffordshire
Gloucestershire	Suffolk
Greater London	Surrey
Greater Manchester	Tyne and Wear
Hampshire	Warwickshire
Herefordshire	West Midlands
Hertfordshire	West Sussex
Isle of Wight	Wiltshire
Kent	Worcestershire

WALES

Clwyd	Mid Glamorgan
Dyfed	Powys
Gwent	South Glamorgan
Gwynedd	West Glamorgan

SCOTLAND

Aberdeenshire	Moray
Angus	Nairn
Argyll and Bute	Orkney
Ayrshire and Arran	Perth and Kinross
Banffshire	Renfrewshire
Berwickshire	Ross
Caithness	Roxburgh, Ettrick
Clackmann	and Lauderdale
Dumfries	Shetland
Dunbartonshire	Stewarty of
East Lothian	Kirkcudbright
Fife	Stirling and Falkirk
Inverness	Sutherland
Kincardineshire	Tweeddale
Lanarkshire	West Lothian
Midlothian	Western Isles
Wigtown	

NORTHERN IRELAND

Co Antrim	Co Fermanagh
Co Armagh	Co Londonderry
Belfast City	Londonderry City
Co Down	Co Tyrone

LORD-LIEUTENANT	There is no specific form of address, but correspondence may be addressed: Colonel Sir John Brown, KCB, DSO, HM Lord-Lieutenant of Blankshire.
VICE LORD-LIEUTENANT AND DEPUTY LIEUTENANTS	There is no recognised abbreviation for a Vice Lord-Lieutenant: he/she continues to use DL after their name. All Deputy Lieutenants are entitled to use the initial DL after their name, but there is no formal way of addressing them.
HIGH SHERIFF	High Sheriffs are appointed for each of the regions listed in England, Wales and Northern Ireland.
SHERIFF: CITY OF LONDON	A sheriff who is also an alderman is addressed according to rank, or as 'sheriff'. When writing in official capacity, the beginning of a letter is 'Dear Alderman and Sheriff'. The envelope to a man is addressed to, for example, 'Mr Alderman and Sheriff Smith' or 'Alderman and Sheriff Sir John Brown'. For a woman, the envelope is addressed to, for example, 'Miss/Mrs/Ms Alderman and Sheriff White' or 'Alderman and Sheriff Lady Green'. Verbally, a sheriff is addressed by name.
SHERIFF: OTHER CITIES	There is no special form of address, but the appointment may follow the name in official correspondence.
UNDER-SHERIFF	There is no specific form of address but in official correspondence, the appointment is included after the name, e.g. Brigadier John Jones, Under-Sheriff of Cheshire.
LORD MAYORS	In Greater London, the following are elected: The Lord Mayor of London, The Lord Mayor of Westminster, The Mayor of London, The Mayor of the Royal Borough of Kensington and Chelsea, The Mayor of the Royal Borough of Kingston-upon-Thames and The Mayor of the 29 remaining boroughs. Elsewhere, the following elect lord mayors: Belfast, Birmingham, Bradford, Bristol, Cardiff, Coventry, Kingston-upon-Hull, Leeds, Leicester, Liverpool, Manchester, Newcastle-upon-Tyne, Norwich, Nottingham, Oxford, Plymouth, Portsmouth, Sheffield, Stoke-on-Trent, York. The Lord Mayors of Belfast, Cardiff, London, Westminster and York are styled The Right Honourable. The remainder are usually styled The Right Worshipful. There is no difference in the form of address for a female Lord Mayor.
DEPUTY LORD MAYOR	The rules for addressing a Lord Mayor apply, but he/she is styled neither Right Honourable, nor Right Worshipful. The verbal address is 'Deputy Lord Mayor'.

MAYORS	The following elect mayors: Bath, Cambridge, Canterbury, Carlisle, Chester, Derby, Durham, Exeter, Gloucester, Hereford, Lancaster, Lincoln, Londonderry, Peterborough, St Albans, Salford, Southampton, Swansea, Wakefield, Winchester, Worcester.
	A mayor of a city is styled The Right Worshipful. Additionally, the Mayors of Dover, Hastings, Hythe, New Romney and Sandwich, the ancient Cinque Ports, are also styled in this way.
	Other mayors are styled as The Worshipful. The use of Your Worship for a mayor is archaic but, if more than one mayor is present, Your Worships is used.
DEPUTY MAYORS OR MAYORESSES	A deputy mayor/mayoress is styled as for a mayor/mayoress, with the addition of 'deputy', but without The Right Worshipful or The Worshipful.
CONSORTS	A lord mayor's or mayor's consort (a lady lord mayor's or mayor's husband) are addressed by name.
HONORARY ALDERMAN	Honorary aldermen are addressed as for an Esquire, or appropriate rank, except that on the envelope 'Honorary Alderman' may follow the name.
CIVIC HEADS: SCOTLAND	The District Councils of Aberdeen, Dundee, Edinburgh and Glasgow elect Lord Provosts. The Lord Provosts of Edinburgh and Glasgow are styled The Right Honourable. Other District Councils elect a Provost, a Chairman or a Convenor.
	The beginning of a formal letter is 'My Lord Provost', 'Dear Provost', 'Dear (Mr or Madam) Chairman' or 'Dear Convenor'. Socially, it is 'Dear Lord Provost'. There is no difference in the form of address for a lady Lord Provost.
	The envelope is addressed to 'The Rt Hon the Lord Provost of Edinburgh', 'The Lord Provost of Aberdeen', 'The Provost of X', 'The Chairman of X' or 'The Convenor of X'. Verbally, he is styled 'Provost', 'Chairman' etc.
	The wife (or lady consort) of a Lord Provost is styled The Lady Provost. The Lady Provosts of Edinburgh and Glasgow are not styled The Right Honourable. The beginning of a letter is 'Dear Lady Provost' and the envelope 'The Lady Provost of X'. Verbally, she is styled 'Lady Provost'.

NAME & PLACECARD	SALUTATION	ENVELOPE	VERBAL ADDRESS
Chairman of a County Council	Dear Chairman (even if a woman)	The Chairman of X County Council	Chairman (even if a woman)
Lord (and Lady) Mayor Placecard: Lord Mayor	Dear Lord Mayor	The Right Honourable the Lord Mayor of X or The Right Worshipful the Lord Mayor of X (check individual circumstances)	My Lord Mayor or Lord Mayor
Lady Mayoress (usually wife or daughter of a mayor) Placecard: Lady Mayoress	Dear Lady Mayoress	The Lady Mayoress of X	Lady Mayoress
Consort of Lady Mayor Placecard: Mr David Howden	Dear Mr Howden	David Howden, Esq	Mr Howden
Mayor Placecard: Mayor of X	Dear Mr or Madam Mayor	The Right Worshipful the Mayor of X or The Worshipful the Mayor of X (check individual circumstances)	Mr or Madam Mayor
Alderman Placecard: Alderman Smith	Dear Alderman or by name	Men: Mr Alderman Smith/Alderman Sir David Smith/Alderman the Rt Hon the Lord Smith/Major and Alderman Smith (also correct for women who may also be styled Mrs or Miss Alderman, followed by her name)	Men: Alderman, which may be followed by the name, and where applicable, title. Women: Alderman, which may be followed by her name, preceded by Mrs or Miss or, where applicable, her title
City, Borough or District Councillor	Dear Councillor (followed by name, preceded, where applicable, by rank and title or in the case of a woman, by Mrs/Miss but not Ms)	Councillor (followed by name, preceded where applicable by rank and title or in the case of a woman, by Mrs/Miss but not Ms)	Councillor (followed by name, where applicable by rank and title or in the case of a woman, by Mrs/Miss but not Ms)

Appendices

Tables of Precedence

GENERAL TABLE OF PRECEDENCE IN ENGLAND AND WALES

The Queen
The Duke of Edinburgh
The Prince of Wales
The Sovereign's younger sons
The Sovereign's grandsons (according to the seniority of their royal parent)
The Sovereign's cousins (according to the seniority of their royal parent)
Archbishop of Canterbury
Lord High Chancellor
Archbishop of York
The Prime Minister
Lord High Treasurer (when existing)
Lord President of the Council
Speaker of the House of Commons
Lord Privy Seal
Ambassadors and High Commissioners
Lord Great Chamberlain
Lord High Constable (when existing) *
Earl Marshal *
Lord Steward of the Household *
Lord Chamberlain of the Household *
Master of the Horse
Dukes of England
Dukes of Scotland
Dukes of Great Britain
Dukes of Ireland
Dukes of the United Kingdom
Eldest sons of Dukes of the Blood Royal (when they are not brothers, grandsons, uncles or nephews of the reigning sovereign)
Marquesses of England
Marquesses of Scotland
Marquesses of Great Britain
Marquesses of Ireland
Marquesses of the United Kingdom
Eldest sons of Dukes
Earls of England
Earls of Scotland
Earls of Great Britain
Earls of Ireland
Earls of the United Kingdom
Younger sons of Dukes of the Blood Royal
Eldest sons of Marquesses
Younger sons of Dukes
Viscounts of England
Viscounts of Scotland
Viscounts of Great Britain
Viscounts of Ireland
Viscounts of the United Kingdom
Eldest sons of Earls
Younger sons of Marquesses
Bishop of London
Bishop of Durham
Bishop of Winchester
English Diocesan Bishops (according to date of consecration)
Suffragan Bishops (according to date of consecration)
Secretaries of State (if of Baronial rank)
Barons of England
Lords of Parliament of Scotland
Barons of Great Britain
Barons of Ireland
Barons of the United Kingdom
Lords of Appeal in Ordinary
Commissioners of the Great Seal (when existing)
Treasurer of the Household
Comptroller of the Household
Vice-Chamberlain of the Household
Secretaries of State (under Baronial rank)
Eldest sons of Viscounts
Younger sons of Earls
Eldest sons of Barons or Lords of Parliament
Knights of the Garter
Privy Counsellors
Chancellor of the Exchequer
Chancellor of the Duchy of Lancaster
Lord Chief Justice
Master of the Rolls
President of the Family Division
Vice-Chancellor of the Chancery Division
Lords Justices of Appeal (according to date of appointment)
Judges of the High Court of Justice (according to date of appointment)
Younger sons of Viscounts
Younger sons of Barons or Lords of Parliament
Younger sons of Life Peers and Lords of Appeal in Ordinary
Baronets

Knights of the Thistle
Knights Grand Cross of the Order of the Bath
Knights Grand Commander of the Order of the Star of India
Knights Grand Cross of the Order of St Michael and St George
Knights Grand Commander of the Order of the Indian Empire
Knights Grand Cross of the Royal Victorian Order
Knights Grand Cross of the Order of the British Empire
Knights Commander of the Order of the Bath
Knights Commander of the Order of the Star of India
Knights Commander of the Order of St Michael and St George
Knights Commander of the Order of the Indian Empire
Knights Commander of the Royal Victorian Order
Knights Commander of the Order of the British Empire
Knights Bachelor
Circuit Judges
Masters in Chancery
Master of Court of Protection
Companions of the Order of the Bath
Companions of the Order of the Star of India
Companions of the Order of St Michael and St George
Companions of the Order of the Indian Empire
Companions of the Royal Victorian Order
Commanders of the Order of the British Empire
Companions of the Distinguished Service Order
Lieutenants of the Royal Victorian Order
Officers o f the Order of the British Empire
Companions of the Imperial Service Order
Eldest sons of the younger sons of Peers
Eldest sons of Baronets
Eldest sons of Knights (according to the precedence of their fathers)
Members of the Royal Victorian Order
Members of the Order of the British Empire
Younger sons of Baronets
Younger sons of Knights
Esquires
Gentlemen

all above peerages of their own degree

PRECEDENCE AMONG LADIES IN ENGLAND AND WALES

The Queen
The Sovereign's daughter
The Sovereign's granddaughters
The Sovereign's cousin
The wife of the Sovereign's eldest son
The wives of the Sovereign's younger sons
The wives of the Sovereign's cousins
The Prime Minister (if female)
Duchesses of England
Duchesses of Scotland
Duchesses of Great Britain
Duchesses of Ireland
Duchesses of the United Kingdom
Wives of the eldest sons of Dukes of the Blood Royal
Marchionesses of England
Marchionesses of Scotland
Marchionesses of Great Britain
Marchionesses of Ireland
Marchionesses of the United Kingdom
Wives of the eldest sons of Dukes
Daughters of Dukes
Countesses of England
Countesses of Scotland
Countesses of Great Britain
Countesses of Ireland
Countesses of the United Kingdom
Wives of the younger sons of Dukes of the Blood Royal
Wives of the eldest sons of Marquesses
Daughters of Marquesses
Wives of the younger sons of Dukes
Viscountesses of England
Viscountesses of Scotland
Viscountesses of Great Britain
Viscountesses of Ireland
Viscountesses of the United Kingdom
Wives of the eldest sons of Earls
Daughters of Earls
Wives of the younger sons of Marquesses
Baronesses of England
Baronesses of Scotland
Baronesses of Great Britain
Baronesses of Ireland
Baronesses of the United Kingdom
Wives of the eldest sons of Viscounts
Daughters of Viscounts
Wives of the younger sons of Earls

Wives of the eldest sons of Barons or Lords of Parliament

Daughters of Barons or Lords of Parliament

Ladies of the Garter

Wives of Knights of the Garter

Privy Counsellors

Wives of the younger sons of Viscounts

Wives of the younger sons of Barons or Lords of Parliament

Daughters of Lords of Appeal

Wives of the sons of Law Lords

Wives of Baronets

Wives of Knights of the Thistle

Dames Grand Cross of the Order of the Bath

Dames Grand Cross of the Order of St Michael and St George

Dames Grand Cross of the Royal Victorian Order

Dames Grand Cross of the Order of the British Empire

Wives of Knights Grand Cross of the Order of the Bath

Wives of Knights Grand Commander of the Order of the Star of India

Wives of Knights Grand Cross of the Order of St Michael and St George

Wives of Knights Grand Commander of the Order of the Indian Empire

Wives of Knights Grand Cross of the Royal Victorian Order

Wives of Knights Grand Cross of the Order of the British Empire

Dames Commander of the Order of the Bath

Dames Commander of the Order of St Michael and St George

Dames Commander of the Royal Victorian Order

Dames Commander of the Order of the British Empire

Wives of Knights Commander of the Order of the Bath

Wives of Knights Commander of the Order of the Star of India

Wives of Knights Commander of the Order of St Michael and St George

Wives of Knights Commander of the Order of the Indian Empire

Wives of Knights Commander of the Royal Victorian Order

Wives of Knights Commander of the Order of British Empire

Wives of Knights Bachelor

Companions of the Order of the Bath

Companions of the Order of St Michael and St George

Commanders of the Royal Victorian Order

Commanders of the Order of the British Empire

Wives of Companions of the Order of the Bath

Wives of Companions of the Order of the Star of India

Wives of Companions of the Order of St Michael and St George

Wives of Companions of the Order of the Indian Empire

Wives of Commanders of the Royal Victorian Order

Wives of Commanders of the Order of the British Empire

Wives of Companions of the Distinguished Service Order

Lieutenants of the Royal Victorian Order

Officers of the Order of the British Empire

Wives of Officers of the Order of the British Empire

Wives of Companions of the Imperial Service Order

Wives of the eldest sons of the younger sons of Peers

Daughters of the younger sons of Peers

Wives of the eldest sons of Baronets

Daughters of Baronets

Wives of the eldest sons of Knights of the Garter

Wives of the eldest sons of Knights

Daughters of Knights

Members of the Royal Victorian Order

Members of the Order of the British Empire

Wives of Members of the Royal Victorian Order

Wives of Members of the Order of the British Empire

Wives of the younger sons of Baronets

Wives of the younger sons of Knights

Wives of Esquires

Wives of Gentlemen

GENERAL TABLE OF PRECEDENCE IN SCOTLAND

The Duke of Edinburgh

Lord High Commissioner to the General Assembly of the Church of Scotland (during sitting of the General Assembly)

Duke of Rothesay (The Prince of Wales)

The Sovereign's younger sons

The Sovereign's grandsons

The Sovereign's nephew

Lord-Lieutenants of counties

Lord Provosts of cities being ex officio Lord-Lieutenants

Sheriffs Principal

Lord Chancellor of Great Britain

Moderator of the General Assembly of the Church of Scotland (during office)

Keeper of the Great Seal of Scotland (The First Minister)

The Presiding Officer

The Secretary of State for Scotland

Hereditary High Constable for Scotland

Hereditary Master of the Household in Scotland

Dukes (as in English Table)

Eldest sons of Dukes of the Blood Royal

Marquesses (as in English Table)

Eldest sons of Dukes

Earls (as in English Table)

Younger sons of Dukes of the Blood Royal

Eldest sons of Marquesses
Younger sons of Dukes
Lord Justice-General
Lord Clerk Register
Lord Advocate
Lord Justice Clerk
Viscounts (as in English Table)
Eldest sons of Earls
Younger sons of Marquesses
Barons (as in English Table)
Eldest sons of Viscounts
Younger sons of Earls
Eldest sons of Barons
Knights of the Garter
Knights of the Thistle
Privy Counsellors
Senators of the College of Justice (Lords of Session)
Younger sons of Viscounts
Younger sons of Barons
Sons of Law Life Peers
Baronets
Knights of St Patrick
Knights Grand Cross and Knights Grand Commander of
    Orders (as in English Table)
Knights Commander of Orders (as in English Table)
Solicitor-General for Scotland
Lord Lyon King of Arms
Sheriffs Principal (when not within own county)
Knights Bachelor
Sheriffs
Commanders of the Royal Victorian Order
Companions of the Order of the Bath
Thence as in English Table

PRECEDENCE AMONG LADIES IN SCOTLAND

The Queen
The Sovereign's daughter
Wives of the Sovereign's younger sons
The Sovereign's granddaughters
The Sovereign's niece
Wife of the Sovereign's nephew
Duchesses (as in English Table)
Wives of the eldest sons of Dukes of the Blood Royal
Marchionesses (as in English Table)
Wives of the eldest sons of Dukes
Daughters of Dukes
Countesses (as in English Table)
Wives of the younger sons of Dukes of the Blood Royal
Wives of the eldest sons of Marquesses
Daughters of Marquesses
Wives of the younger sons of Dukes
Viscountesses (as in English Table)
Wives of the eldest sons of Earls
Daughters of Earls
Wives of the younger sons of Marquesses
Baronesses (as in English Table)
Wives of the eldest sons of Viscounts
Daughters of Viscounts
Wives of the younger sons of Earls
Wives of the eldest sons of Barons
Daughters of Barons
Maids of Honour of the Queen
Ladies of the Order of the Garter
Wives of Knights of the Garter
Ladies of the Order of the Thistle
Wives of Knights of the Thistle
Wives of the younger sons of Viscounts
Wives of the younger sons of Barons
Daughters of Law Peers (Lords of Appeal in Ordinary)
Wives of the sons of Law Peers (Lords of Appeal in Ordinary)
Wives of Baronets
Wives of Knights of St Patrick
Dames Grand Cross of Orders (as in English Table)
Wives of Knights Grand Cross and Knights Grand Commander of
    Orders (as in English Table)
Dames Commander of Orders (as in English Table)
Wives of Knights Commander of Orders (as in English Table)
Wives of Knights Bachelor and Wives of Senators of the College of
    Justice (Lords of Session)
Wives of Companions of the Order of the Bath
Thence as in English Table

Further Information

Legal Documents

Peers and peeresses (in their own right and the wives/widows of peers) are accorded their full formal styles with their forenames but with no surname. For example: The Most Noble Charles John, Duke of Blank or The Most Noble Anne Frances, Duchess of Blank; The Most Honourable Charles, Marquess (of) Blank or The Most Honourable Anna, Marchioness (of) Blank; The Right Honourable Simon Thomas, Earl (of), Viscount or Baron Blank or The Right Honourable Annabel, Countess (of), Viscountess or Baroness Blank.

Peers with courtesy titles, and their spouses, are not accorded the prefix 'Most Honourable' or 'Right Honourable'. The latter is used only if they are also members of the Privy Council. The full description is John Mulgrave Esquire, commonly called Lord John Mulgrave or Emily Addison Spinster, commonly called the Honourable Emily Addison. In practice, however, the use of the courtesy title only, such as John Brandon, Viscount Hammersmith, is generally considered sufficient.

Baronets are accorded 'Baronet' after their name. Knights bachelor are accorded 'Knight Bachelor' or 'Knight'. Membership etc. of Orders of Chivalry is either spelt in full, with or without the honorific prefix of the order (i.e. the Most Excellent Order of the British Empire), or with the abbreviation, such as DBE.

The listing of names on share certificates largely follows the same principles as for legal documents. Dukes and Duchesses may be described by the slightly less formal 'His (or Her) Grace'. Surnames are never used.

Every passport includes a person's forenames as a means of identification. Passports for peers have the appropriate abbreviated prefix before the title, which is followed by any postnominal letters. The forenames appear underneath.

Plaques and Memorials

Inscriptions upon plaques and memorials – i.e. gravestones – usually include all forenames and the surname. For a peer, all of the forenames are included, with or without the appropriate prefix. If the prefix is used, it is generally given in full, such as 'The Most Honourable'. A peer's surname and the territorial designation can also be used. A peer or baronet is sometimes numbered. For example: John George Miles Heinemann, 8th Duke of Blankshire.

Postnominal letters denoting orders, decorations and degrees may also be included. It is also a matter of choice as to whether coats of arms are to be displayed. If there is any doubt about their accuracy, reference should be made to the College of Arms or, for Scottish families, to the Lord Lyon King of Arms.

Colleges

Heads of House of Oxford and Cambridge colleges and permanent private halls:

MASTER

Christ's College, Cambridge

Churchill College, Cambridge

Clare College, Cambridge

Corpus Christi College, Cambridge

Downing College, Cambridge

Emmanuel College, Cambridge

Fitzwilliam College, Cambridge

Gonville & Caius College, Cambridge

Jesus College, Cambridge

Magdalene College, Cambridge

Pembroke College, Cambridge

Peterhouse, Cambridge

Queens' College, Cambridge

St Catharine's College, Cambridge

St Edmund's College, Cambridge

St John's College, Cambridge

Selwyn College, Cambridge

Sidney Sussex College, Cambridge

Trinity College, Cambridge

Trinity Hall, Cambridge

Darwin College, Cambridge

Balliol College, Oxford

Pembroke College, Oxford

St Catherine's College, Oxford

St Peter's College, Oxford

University College, Oxford

Campion Hall, Oxford

St Benet's Hall, Oxford

St Cross College, Oxford

PRINCIPAL

Homerton College, Cambridge

Newnham College, Cambridge

Brasenose College, Oxford

Corpus Christi College, Oxford

Harris Manchester College, Oxford

Hertford College, Oxford

Jesus College, Oxford

Lady Margaret Hall, Oxford

Mansfield College, Oxford

St Anne's College, Oxford

St Edmund Hall, Oxford

St Hilda's College, Oxford

St Hugh's College, Oxford

Somerville College, Oxford

Regent's Park College, Oxford

St Stephen's House, Oxford

Wycliffe Hall, Oxford

Linacre College, Oxford

PRESIDENT

Hughes Hall, Cambridge

Lucy Cavendish College, Cambridge

New Hall, Cambridge

Wolfson College, Cambridge

Clare Hall, Cambridge

Magdalen College, Oxford

St John's College, Oxford

Trinity College, Oxford

Kellogg College, Oxford

Wolfson College, Oxford

Regent

Blackfriars Hall, Oxford

Mistress

Girton College, Cambridge

Rector

Exeter College, Oxford

Lincoln College, Oxford

WARDEN

Robinson College, Cambridge

Keble College, Oxford

Merton College, Oxford

New College, Oxford

Wadham College, Oxford

Greyfriars Hall, Oxford

All Souls College, Oxford

Green College, Oxford

Nuffield College, Oxford

Dean

Christ Church, Oxford

Templeton College, Oxford

Provost

King's College, Cambridge

Oriel College, Oxford

The Queen's College, Oxford

Worcester College, Oxford

Pronounciation of Titles and Surnames

SURNAME	PRONUNCIATION
Abercrombie	Aber-crum-by (sometimes pronounced as spelt)
Abergavenny	Aber-*genny* (title – town pronounced as spelt)
Abinger	Abin-jer
Acheson	Atchesson
Adye	Aydi
Aldous	*All*-dus
Alleyne	Alleen (sometimes pronounced as spelt)
Alnwick	Annick
Althorp	*All*-thorp (since 2000, previously *All*-trup)
Altrincham	Altringham
Alvingham	All-ving-am
Alman	Amman
Ampthill	Ampt-hill
Annesley	*Anns*-li
Apethorpe	App-thorp
Arbuthnot, Arbuthnott	A-*buth*-not
Ardee	A-*dee*
Arundel	*Arun*-del
Ashburnham	Ash-*burn*-am
Assheton	Ash-ton
Atholl	*Uh*-thol *or Ah*-thol
Auchinleck	Affleck *or Ock*-inleck
Audley	*Awd*-li
Ava	Ah-va
Ayscough	Askew

SURNAME	PRONUNCIATION
Babington	*Babb*-ington
Baden-Powell	Bayden-Poell
Bagot	*Bag*-ot
Balcarres	Bal-*carris*
Balogh	Balog ('Bal' as in 'Hal')
Bampfylde	*Bam*-field
Baring	*Bear*-ing
Barnardiston	Bar-nar-*dis*-ton
Barttelot	Bartlot
Basing	Bayzing
Bathurst	*Bath*-urst ('a' as in 'cat')
Bazalgette	Bazl-jet
Beauchamp	Beecham
Beauclerk	Bo-clare
Beaudesert	Bodezair
Beaufort	*Bo*-foot
Beaulieu	*Bew*-ley
Beaumont	Bo-mont

Becher	Beacher
Bechervaise	*Besh*-er-vayse
Bedingfield	Beddingfield
Behrens	Barens
Belfast	Bel-*fast*
Bellew	*Bell*-ew
Bellingham	Bellingjam *or* Bellingum
Belvoir	Beevor
Bengough	Ben-*goff*
Beresford	*Berris*-fud
Berkeley	Barkli
Bertie	Barti
Betham	*Bee*-tham
Bethune	Beaton
Bicester	Bister
Blakiston	Blackiston
Bledisloe	Bledslow
Blenheim	*Blen*-im
Bligh	Bly
Blithfield	Bliffield
Blois	Bloyss
Blomefield	Bloomfield
Blount	Blunt
Blyth	Bly
Boevey	Boovey *or* Buvey (short 'u')
Boleyn	*Bull*-in
Bolingbroke	*Bulling*-brook
Boord	Board
Boreel	Borale
Borrowes	Burrows
Borwick	Borrick
Bosham	*Bos*-am
Bosanquet	*Bozen*-ket
Boscawen	Bos-*cowen*
Botetourt	Botti-tort
Boughey	Boey
Boughton	Bought-on (village pronounced 'Bough-ton')
Bourchier	*Bough*-cher
Bourke	Burke
Bourne	Boorn
Bowden	Bowden (as in 'no')
Bowes	Bose (to rhyme with 'rose')
Bowman	Boman
Bowyer	Bo-yer (as in 'no')
Brabazon	*Brab*-azon
Brabourne	*Bray*-burn
Breadalbane	Bread-*auburn*
Breitmeyer	Bright-mire
Brereton	Breer-ton
Brise	Brize
Brocas	Brockas

Name	Pronunciation
Broke	Brook (HMS *Broke* as spelt)
Bromhead	Brumhead
Brougham	Broom *or* Brooham
Broughton	Brawton
Broun	Brune
Bruntisfield	Bruntsfield
Brynkir	Brinkeer
Buccleuch	Bu-*cloo*
Bulkeley	Buckley
Burgh	Borough
Burghersh	Burg-ish
Burghley	Ber-li
Bury	Berry (England), Bure-y (Ireland)
Caccia	Catch a
Cadogan	Ka-*dugan*
Caius	Keys (Cambridge college)
Caldecote	Call-di-cot
Calderon	*Call*-dron
Callaghan	*Calla*-han
Calver	Carver
Calverley	*Car*-verly *or* *Calf*-ley
Camoys	Cam-oyz
Capell	*Cayple*
Carew	As spelt (Cary has become archaic)
Calthorpe	*Call*-thorpe (Cal-trop has become archaic)
Carnegie	Car-*neggie*
Carteret	*Carter*-et
Cassilis	Cassels
Castlereagh	*Castle*-ray
Carthcart	Cath-*cart*
Cathie	*Cay*-thie
Cato	*Kate*-o
Cator	Cay-tor
Caulfield	*Caw*-field
Cavan	*Cav*-en ('a' as in 'cat')
Cavanagh	*Cava*-na
Cecil	Cicil
Chandos	Shandos
Charlemont	Shar-le-mont
Charteris	As spelt (Charters is archaic)
Chattan	Hattan
Chenevix	*Sheeni*vix *or* *Shenn*evy
Chernocke	Char-nock
Chetwode	Chetwood
Chetwynd	Chetwind
Cheylesmore	*Chyles*-more
Cheyne	Chain, Chainy *or* Cheen
Chichele	*Chich*-ley
Chisholm	*Chis*-um
Cholmeley, Cholmondeley	*Chum*-li
Cilcennin	Kil-*kennin*
Claverhouse	Clayvers
Clerk	Clark
Cloete	Clootie
Clough	Cluff
Clowes	Clues
Clwyd	*Cloo*-id
Cochrane	*Coch*-ran
Cockburn	*Co*-burn
Coghlan	Co-lan
Coke	Cook (sometimes as spelt)
Coleraine	Cole-*rain*
Colquhoun	Ca-hoon
Colville	*Col*-ville *or* Col-ville
Combe	Coom
Combermere	*Cumber*-mere
Compton	Cumpton
Conesford	*Connis*-ford
Conolly	*Con*-olly
Constable	*Cun*-stable
Conyngham, Conynghame	Cunningham
Cosham	As spelt
Cottenham	*Cot*-nam
Cottesloe	*Cots*-low
Couchman	Cowchman
Courthope	Cort-hope
Cowper	Cooper
Cozens	Cuzzens
Cracroft	*Cray*-croft
Craigavon	Craig-*avv*-on
Craster	Crarster
Creagh	Cray
Creighton	Cryton
Crespigny	*Crepp*-ni
Crichton	Cryton
Cromartie	*Crum*-aty
Crombie	Crumbie
Culme	Cullum (Sometimes as spelt)
Cuming	Cumming
Cunynghame	Cunningham
D'Abrell	*Dab*-roo
Dacre	Dayker
Dalbiac	*Dawl*-biac
Dalhousie	Dal-*howsi*
Dalmeny	Dul-*menny*
Dalyell	Dee-el *or* Dayli-el
Dalzell	Dee-el *or* Dayli-el
Darcy de Knayth	Darcy de Nayth
Daresbury	Darsbury
Daubeney	*Daub*-ny
Daventry	As spelt ('Daintry' is archaic)
Davies	Davis
De Blacquiere	De *Black*-yer
De Burgh	De Burg
Decies	Deeshies

De Courcy	De Koursey	Elphinstone	*Elfin*-ston
De Crespigny	De *Crepp*-ni	Elveden	*Elve*-den (Place 'Elden')
De Freyne	De *Frain*	Elwes	*El*-wes
De Hoghton	De Hawton	Erle	Earl
De la Warr	Della-ware	Ernle	Earnley
Delamere	Della-mare	Erskine	*Ers*-kin
De la Poer	De la *Poor*	Eveleigh	*Eve*-ley
De la Rue	Della-rue	Eyre	Air
De L'Isle	De Lyle	Every	As spelt
De Lotbiniere	De Lobin-yare	Eyton	*I*-tun
De Moleyns	*Demo*-lins		
Dering	*Deer*-ing		
De Ros	De *Roos*		
Derwent	Darwent	Falconer	Fawkner
De Salis	De Saals *or* De Sal-is	Falkiner	Fawkner
Devereux	Dev-rooks *or* Dever-oo	Faringdon	Farringdon
De Vesci	De Vessy	Farquhar	Farkwar
De Villiers	De Villers	Farquharson	Farkwerson
Diomede	Di-o-meed	Fayrer	*Fair*-er
Dilhorne	*Dill*'n	Featherstonhaugh	Fetherston-haugh
Dominguez	Dum-*ing*-ez		*or* Fetherston
Doneraile	Dunnaral	Feilding	*Field*-ing
Donoughmore	Duno-more	Fenwick	*Fenn*-ick
Doune	Doun	Fergussen	Ferguson
Douro	*Dur*-o	Fermor	Farmer
Drogheda	*Droyi*-da	Feversham	Fevver-sham (Place
Drumalbyn	Drum-*albin*		'Favversham')
Duchesnes	Du *Karn(s)* (sometimes	ffolliott	*Foll*-y-ot
	French 'Du-shayn'	ffolkes	Foaks
Ducie	*Dew*-si	Fiennes	Fines
Du Cros	Du *Crow*	Fingall	Fin-*gawl*
Dukinfield	*Duckin*-field	Fitzhardinge	Fitzharding
Dumaresq	Du-*merrick*	Foljambe	Full-jum
Dunally	Dun-*alley*	Forestier	Forest-tier
Dundas	Dun-*das*	Fortuin	Fortayne
Dungarvan	Dun-*gar*-van	Foulis	Fowls
Dunglass	Dun-*glass*	Fowke	Foke
Dunsany	Dun-*saney*	Fremantle	*Free*-mantle
Duntze	Dunts	Freyburg	*Fry*-burg
Du Plat	Du-Pla	Froude	Frood
Dupplin	*Dupp*-lin	Furneaux	*Fur*-no
Durand	*Du*-rand *or* Dur-*rand*		
Dymoke	Dimmock		
Dynevor	*Dinny*-yer		
Dysart	Dy-z't	Gairdner	Gardner
		Galston	*Gaul*-ston
		Galway	Gaulway
		Garioch	Gary (to rhyme with 'Mary'
			or Geary)
Ebury	*Ee*-bri		
Echlin	Eck-lin	Garvagh	*Gar*-va
Edwardes	Edwards	Gathorne	Gaythorn
Egan	*Ee*-gan	Geoghegan	*Gay*-gan
Egerton	*Edger*-ton	Gerrard	Jerrard
Elcho	Elco	Gervis	Jervis
Elgin	El-gin (hard 'g')	Giffard	Jiffard
Elibank	Elli-bank	Gill	As spelt (hard 'g')

Name	Pronunciation	Name	Pronunciation
Gillespie	Gill-*es*-py (hard 'g')	Housman	House-man
Gilmour	Gillmoor (hard 'g')	Howick	Hoyk
Glamis	Glahms	Hugessen	*Hu*-ges-*son* (hard 'g')
Glasgow	*Glass*-go	Huth	Hooth
Glenavy	Glen-*avy* (as in 'day')	Hylton	Hilton
Glerawly	Gler-*awly*		
Gorges	Gorjes		
Gormanstown	*Gor*-mans-ton		
Goschen	*Go*-shen	Iddesleigh	*Idd*-sli
Gough	Goff	Ikerrin	I-kerrin
Goulding	Goolding	Iliffe	I-liffe
Gower	Gore (place names as spelt	Inchiquin	Inch-quin
Graeme	Grame (to rhyme with 'frame')	Inchrye	Inch-rye
Grantham	*Gran*-tham	Inchyra	Inch-*eye*-ra
Greaves	Graves	Inge	Ing
Greig	Gregg	Ingestre	Ingustry (like 'industry')
Grosvenor	*Grove*-nor	Inglis	Ingles *or* as spelt
Guise	Gyze	Inigo	*Inni*-go
Gwynedd	*Gwinn*-eth	Innes	Inniss
		Inveraray	Inver-*air*-a
		Ionides	Ion-*ee*-diz
		Isham	I-sham
		Iveagh	I-va
Haden-Guest	Hayden-Gest (hard 'g')		
Haldane	*Hall*-dane		
Halsey	*Hall*-sey		
Halsbury	*Halls*-bry	Jervis	As spelt *or* Jarvis
Hamond	Hammond	Jervoise	Jervis
Harcourt	*Har*-cut	Jocelyn	Josslin
Hardinge	Harding	Jolliffe	*Joll*-iff
Harewood	*Har*-wood (village pronounced Hare-wood)		
Harington	Harrington		
Harwich	Harrich		
Hawarden	*Hay*-warden	Kaberry	*Kay*-berry
Haworth	*Hay*-worth (Harden for title is archaic)	Kavenagh	*Kavan*-a
		Kekewich	*Keck*-which
Heathcoat	Heth-cut	Keighley	*Keith*-li
Heathcote	Heth-cut	Kemeys	Kemmis
Heneage	Hennidge	Kennard	Ken-*ard*
Hepburn	*Heb*-b'n	Kenyon	*Ken*-yon
Herschell	Her-shell	Ker, Kerr	Car *or* Cur
Hertford	*Har*-ford	Keynes	Kaynes
Hervey	Harvey	Killanin	Kil-*lah*-nin
Hever	Heaver	Kilmorey	Kil-*murray*
Heytesbury	*Hetts*-b'ry	Kingsale	King-*sale*
Heywood	Haywood	Kinnoull	Kin-*ool*
Hindlip	*Hynd*-lip	Kirkcudbright	Cuck-*coo*-bri
Hippesley	*Hips*-ley	Knollys	Nowles
Hobart	Hubbard (city as spelt)	Kylsant	Kill-*sant*
Hogan	*Ho*-gan	Knyvett	Nivett
Holbech	*Hole*-beech		
Home	Hume		
Honywood	Honeywood		
Hopetoun	Hopetown	Lacon	*Lay*-kon
Horsbrugh	Horsbro	Laffan	Laf-*fan*
Hotham	*Huth*-am	Lamplugh	*Lamp*-loo

Name	Pronunciation
Lascelles	*Lass*-ells
Lathom	*Lay*-thom
LaTouche	La *Toosh*
Latymer	Latimer
Laurie	Lorry
Layard	Laird
Leacock	Laycock *or* Leccock
Lechmere	Letchmere
Le Fanu	*Leff*-new
Lefevre	Le-*fever*
Legard	Le-jard
Legh	Lee
Leighton	Layton
Leinster	Linster
Leitrim	Leetrim
Le Mesurier	Le *Mezz*-erer
Leominster	Lemster
Leven	*Lee*-ven
Leverhulme	*Leaver*-hulme
Leveson-Gower	Loosun-Gore
Levinge	As spelt (hard 'g')
Levy	Levvy *or* Levi
Ley	Lay *or* Lee
Leycester	Lester
Liardet	Lee-ardet
Liddell	*Lid*-el
Lisle	Lyle
Listowel	Lis-*toe*-ell
Lombe	Loam (sometimes Lumb)
Londesborough	Londs-bro'
Londonderry	*Londond'*ry (city pronounced London-Derry
Loudon	*Loud*-on
Loughborough	*Luff*-bro
Louth	'th' as in 'mouth' (Ireland 'th' as in 'breathe')
Lovat	Luv-at
Lowson	Lo-son ('lo' as in 'go')
Lowther	*Low*-thr ('low' as in 'now')
Lycett	Lisset
Lygon	Liggon
Lyon	Lion
Lysaght	Ly-set
Lyveden	*Live*-den (as in 'give')
Macara	Mac-*ara*
Macbean	Mac-*bain*
McCorquodale	M'*cork*-o-dale
McCulloch	M'*cull*-och
McDonagh	Mac-Donna
McEvoy	Mac-evoy
McEwan	Mac-*ewen*
McFadzean	Mac *fadd*-yen
McGillycuddy	*Mac*-li-*cuddy*

Name	Pronunciation
Machell	*May*-chell
McIvor	Mac-*Ivor*
McKay	M'*Kye* (as in 'eye')
McKie	*Mack*-ie (occasionally pronounced M'*Kye*)
Maclean	Mac-*layne*
Macleay	Mac-*lay*
Macleod	Mac-*loud*
McLachlan	Mac-*lochlan*
Macnaghten	Mac-*nawton*
Macmahon	Mac-*mahn*
Maelor	Myla
Magdala	Mag-*dahla*
Magdalen, Magdalene	Maudlin
Magrath	Ma-*grah*
Mahon	Mahn *or* Ma-*han*
Mahony	*Mah*-ni
Mainwaring	*Manner*-ing
Mais	Mayz
Majendic	Ma-*jendy*
Makgill	Mc-*gill* (hard 'g')
Malpas	*Mawl*-pas
Malet	Mallet
Malmsbury	*Marms*-bri
Mandeville	Mande-ville (first 'e' slightly inflected)
Mander	Mahnder
Mansergh	Manser
Margesson	*Mar*-jesson
Marjoribanks	Marchbanks
Marlborough	*Maul*-bro
Marquand	Mark-wand
Martineau	Martinowe
Masham	*Mass*-ham
Masserene	Mazereen
Mathias	Math-*ias*
Maughan	Mawm
Mauchline	*Mauch* (as in 'loch')-lynn
Maunsell	*Man*-sel
Maxse	Maxie
Meath	Meeth ('th' as in 'breathe')
Meiklejohn	*Mickel*-john
Melhuish	*Mell*-ish
Menteth	Men-*teeth*
Menzies	Ming-iz
Merioneth	Merry-*on*-eth
Mereworth	*Merry*-worth
Metcalfe	Met-calf
Methuen	Meth-wen
Meux	Mews
Meynell	*Men*-el
Meyrick	Merr-ick
Mitchelham	*Mitch*-lam
Michie	Micky
Midleton	*Middle*-ton
Millais	*Mill*-ay

Mocatta	Mow-*catta*	Paton	Payton
Molyneux	*Mully*-neux *or* Mully-nu	Paulet	*Paul*-et
Monaco	*Mon*-aco	Paunceforte, Pauncefote	*Pawns*-fort
Monck	Munk	Pechell	*Peach*-ell
Monckton	Munkton	Pennefather	*Penn*-ifither *or* Penny-feather
Monro	Mun-*roe*	Pennycuick	*Penny*-cook
Monson	*Mun*-sun	Pepys	Peppis (Peeps has become archaic, except for the diarist and the Pepys Cockerell family)
Montagu	*Mon*-tagu		
Montgomery, Montgomerie	Mun-*gum*-eri		
Monzie	M'*nee*	Perceval	Percival
Moran	Moor-an	Pery	Pairy
Moray	Murray	Peto	*Peet*-o
Mordaunt	*Mor*-dant	Petre	Peter
Mosicy	Mozeley	Petrie	*Peet*-rie
Mostyn	*Moss*-tin	Peyton	Payton
Mottistone	Mottiston	Phayre	Fair
Moulton	*Mole*-ton	Pierpoint	Pierpont
Mountmorres	Mount-morris	Pleydell	Pleddel
Mowbray	*Mo*-bray	Plowden	Ploughden
Mowll	Mole	Plumtre	*Plum*-tri
Moynihan	*Moy*-ni-han	Pole	Pole *or* Pool (see also Carew)
Munro	Mun-*roe*	Poltimore	Pole-ti-more
Myddelton	Middle-ton	Polwarth	*Pol*-worth
Mytton	Mitton	Pomeroy	*Pom*-roy
		Pomfret	*Pum*-fret
		Ponsonby	Punsunby
		Poulett	*Paul*-et
Naas	Nace	Powell	Powell *or* Poell
Naesmyth	*Nay*-smith	Powerscourt	*Poers*-caut
Nall	Nawl	Powis	*Po*-iss
Napier	*Nay*-pier	Powlett	*Paul*-et
Nathan	Naythan	Powys	Po-iss (name) (place pronounced 'Powiss')
Nepean	Ne-*peen*		
Newburgh	*New*-bro'	Praed	Praid
Niven	Nivven	Prevost	*Prev*-o
Northcote	*North*-cut	Prideaux	Priddo
Nunburnholme	Nun-burnham	Puleston	*Pill*-ston
		Purefuy	Pure-foy
		Pytchley	*Pietch*-li
Ochterlony	Ochter-*lony*		
Offaly	*Off*-aly	Quibell	Quy-*bell* (as in 'high')
Ogilvie, Ogilvy	*Ogle*-vi		
O'Hagan	O'*Hay*-gan		
Olivier	O-livier	Raleigh	*Raw*-li
O'Loghlen	O'*Loch*-len	Ranfurly	*Ran*-fully
Ormonde	*Or*-mund	Rankeillour	Rank-illour
O'Rourke	O'Rork	Ratendone	Ratten-dun
Outram	*Oot*-ram	Rathdonnell	Rath-*donnell*
		Rea	Ree
		Rearsby	*Rears*-bi
Pakington	Packington	Reay	Ray
Paget	*Paj*-it	Redesdale	*Reads*-dale
Pakenham	*Pack*-en'um	Renwick	*Renn*-ick
Pasley	*Pais*-li		

Reresby	*Rears*-bi	Segal	Seagal
Reuter	*Roy*-ter	Segrave	Sea-grave
Rhyl	Rill	Sele	Seal
Rhys	Rees *or* Rice	Sempill	Semple
Riddell	*Riddle*	Seton	Seaton
Rideau	*Reed*-owe	Seymour	Seamer *or as spelt*
Roborough	*Roe*-bra'	Shakerley	Shackerley
Roche	Roach *or* Rosh	Shaughnessy	Shawnessy
Roden	Roe-den	Sherborne	Shirb'n
Rolfe	Roaf (as in 'loaf')	Shrewsbury	*Shrows*-b'ry (town has
Rolleston	*Roll*-ston		alternative pronunciation
Romilly	*Rum*-illy		of *Shrews*-b'ry
Romney	Rumney		
Ronaldshay	*Ron*-alld-shay	Shuckburgh	*Shuck*-bro'
Rotherwick	As spelt	Sieff	Seef
Rothes	*Roth*-is	Simey	Symey
Rous, Rouse	Rowse (as in 'grouse')	Skene	Skeen
Rowley	*Roe*-li	Skrine	Screen
Roxburghe	Rox-bro	Smijth	Smyth
Ruabon	Ru-*a*-bon	Smyth	Smith *or* Smythe
Ruthin	Ruth-in	Smythe	Smythe
Ruthven	Rivven	Sneyd	Sneed
		Somers	Summers
		Somerset	Summerset
		Sotheby	*Sutha*-by
		Soulbury	*Sool*-bri
Sacheverall	Sash-*ever*-al	Southwark	*Suth*-erk
Sacheverell	Sash-*ev*-rell	Southwell	*Suth*-ell
St Aubyn	S'nt *Aw*-bin	Sowerby	Sour-by
St Clair	Sinclair *or as spelt*	Spottiswoode	Spotswood
St Cyres	S'nt Sires (to rhyme with 'fires')	Stanhope	Stannup
St John	Sin-jun	Staordale	*Stav*-erdale
St Leger	*Sill*-inger *or* St Leger	Stonor	Stone-er
St Levan	S'nt Leaven (as in 'leaven'	Stourton	Sturton
	for bread)	Strabane	Stra-*bann*
St Maur	S'nt *More*	Strabolgi	Stra-*bogie* (hard 'g')
Salisbury	*Sawls*-bri	Strachan	Strawn
Salkeld	Saul-keld	Straghan	Strawn
Saltoun	*Salt*-on	Strahan	Strawn
Salusbury	*Sawls*-bri	Strachi	*Stray*-chie
Sandbach	Sandbatch	Stratheden	Strath-*eden*
Sandeman	*Sandy*-man	Strathspey	Strath-*spay*
Sandys	Sands	Streatfield	Stret-field
Sanquhar	Sanker (Sanwer is historically	Stucley	*Stewk*-li
	correct)	Suirdale	Sure-dale
Saumarez	Summer-ez *or Saumer*-ez	Sysonby	*Size*-on-by
Sausmarez	Summer-ez *or Saumer*-ez	Synge	Sing
Savernake	Savver-nack		
Savile	Saville		
Saye and Sele	Say and Seal	Talbot	*Tall*-bot
Schilizzi	Skil-it-zy	Tangye	Tang-y
Schuster	*Shoo*-ster	Taverne	Tav-*erne*
Sclater	Slater	Taylour	Taylor
Scone	Scoon	Teignmouth	*Tin*-muth
Scudamore	*Scooda*-more	Terregles	Terry-*glaze*
Scrymgeour	*Scrim*-jer	Teynham	*Ten*-'am
Sedburgh	Sed-ber		

Thame	Tame	Waleran	*Wall*-ran
Thellusson	*Tellus*-son	Walmer	*Wall*-mer
Theobald	Tibbald *or* as spelt	Walrond	*Wall*-rond
Thesiger	*Thesi*-jer	Walsingham	*Wall*-sing'm
Thorold	Thurrald	Walwyn	Wall-wyn
Thynne	Thin	Wathen	Wothen
Tichbourne	*Titch*-bourne	Wauchope	*Walk*-up ('ch' as in 'loch')
Tighe	Tie	Waugh	As spelt, to rhyme with 'flaw'
Tollemache	*Tol*-mash (Tall-mash is archaic)	Wavell	*Way*-vell
Torphichen	Tor-*kken*	Weighall	*Wy*-gall
Touchet	*Touch*-et	Weighill	*Wey*-hill
Tovey	Tuvvy	Wellesley	*Wells*-li
Trafalgar	Traffle-*gar* (title only)	Wemyss	Weems
Traquair	Tra-*quare*	Wernher	Werner
Tredegar	Tre-*deegar*	Westenra	*Westen*-ra
Trefusis	Tre-*fusis*	Westmeath	West-*meath* ('th' as in s'breathe')
Trevelyan	Tre-*villian*		
Trimlestown	*Trimmels*-ton	Westmorland	*West*-morland
Trowbridge	Troobridge	Wharton	*Whor*-ton
Tuchet	*Touch*-et	Wigoder	*Wigg*-oder
Tuite	Tute	Wigram	*Wigg*-ram
Tullibardine	Tulli-*bard*-in	Wilbraham	*Will*-bram
Turnour	Turner	Willoughby de Eresby	*Willow*-bi deersby
Tuvey	Tuvvy	Willoughby de Broke	*Willow*-bi de Brook
Twohy	*Too*-y	Winder	*Winn*-der
Twysden	Twis-den	Woburn	*Woo*-burn
Tynte	Tint	Wodehouse	*Wood*-house
Tyrrell	Tirrell	Wollaston	*Wool*-aston
Tyrwhitt	Tirrit	Wolley	Wooly
Tyzack	*Tie*-sack	Wolmer	*Wool*-mer
		Wolrige	*Wool*-ridge
		Wolseley	*Wool*-sli
		Wombwell	*Woom*-well
Urquhart	*Urk*-ut	Wontner	Wantner
Uvedale	*Youv*-dale	Worsley	*Wers*-li *or* Werz-li
		Wortley	*Wert*-li
		Wriothesley	Rottisli
		Wrottesley	*Rotts*-li
Vachell	*Vay*-chell	Wykeham	*Wick*-am
Valentia	Val-*en*-shia	Wyllie	*Wy*-lie
Valletort	Valley-tort	Wyndham	*Wind*-'am
Van Straubenzee	Van Straw-*ben*-zie	Wynford	*Win*-fud
Vaughan	Vawn	Wynyard	Win-yard
Vaux	Vokes	Wythenshaw	*With*-in-shaw
Vavasour	*Vav*-assur	Yeatman	Yaytman
Verschoyle	Ver-*skoil*	Yerburgh	*Yar*-bra'
Vesey	Veezy	Yonge	Young
Vigor	Vygor		
Villiers	Villers		
Vyvyan	Vivian		
		Zouch	Zooch
Waechter	Vechter (guttural 'ch')		
Wagner	As spelt		
Waldegrave	Waldgrave *or* Wargrave		

Credits

PENS SUPPLIED BY: Cartier

Tel: 020 8080 0330

www.cartier.com

STATIONERY PROVIDED BY: The Wren Press Stationers Ltd

1 Chelsea Wharf, 15 Lots Road, London SW10 0QJ

Tel: 020 7351 5887

www.wrenpress.com

Debrett's would like to thank Nigel Rawlence, Nicky Granville, Sally Mitchell and Luke Lavender

Bibliography

Debrett's Etiquette and Modern Manners by Elsie Burch Donald

Debrett's Guide to Correspondence by Rolf Kurth

Debrett's New Guide to Etiquette and Modern Manners by John Morgan

Manners by Kate Spade

The Smythson Guide to Everyday Stationery

Picture Credits

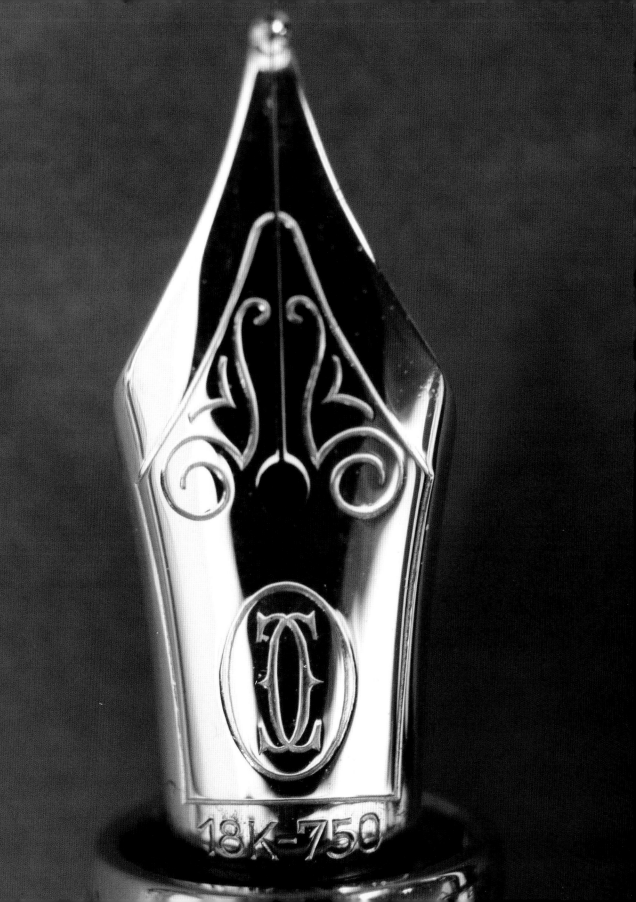

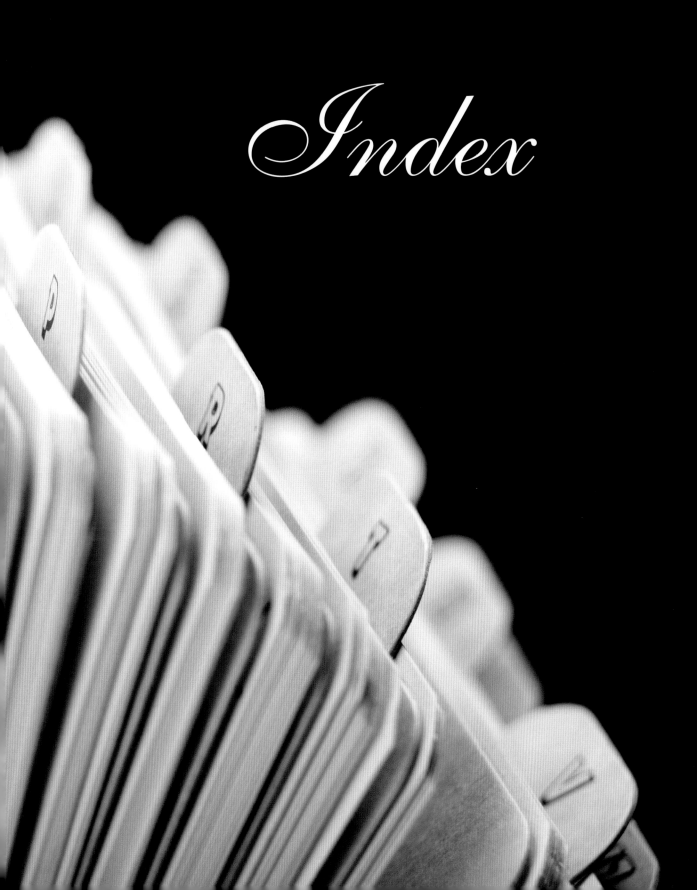

Index

Index

Where more than one page number is listed against a heading, page numbers in bold indicate significant treatment of a subject.

The letter 't' after a page number refers to tables.

abbots 144t

Academicians, Royal 124, 128

academics 146-7

address, change of 121

address, forms of 66-70, **78-107t**

admirals, 148, 149t

admission cards 31, 34

adopted children, of peers 94

adoption cards 112

Aide de Camp to the Queen 124

Air Force, Royal 61, 129, 148, **152t**

Air Force (US) 68

aldermen 59, 161, 162, 163t

alert tones for text messages 16

ambassadors 50, 53, 58, 67, 70t, **153t**

American usage 66-75

Anglican Communion 136-40t

Antiquaries, Society of 127

archbishops 50, 58, 61, 136, **139t**, 142, **143t**

archdeacons 61, 138, 139t

Armed Forces 60, 61, 124, 129, 140, **148-52t**

Armed Forces (US) 68

Army, The British 129, 148, **150-1t**

'At Home' invitations 32, 33

attachments to emails 13

Attorney General (US) 70

Australia, orders and decorations 133

automatic signatures in emails 14

baccalaureates 156

backbenchers 159t

baptisms 113

Baptist Union of GB and Ireland 145

Bar/Bat Mitzvahs 113

baronets and baronetesses 54, 60, **96-7t**
    see also orders of chivalry; The Peerage; The Royal Family

barons and baronesses 92-3t, 94, 95

bereavement 116-17

birth announcements and ceremonies 112-13

bishops 61, 137, **139t**, 142, **143t**

blind copies ('bcc') for emails 13

bowing/curtsying to The Royal Family 81

brigadiers (HM Forces) 151t

Brit milah 113

British Academy 127

British Army, The 129, 148, **150-1t**

business cards 22, 69

business correspondence 12-23
    see also social correspondence

Cabinet Ministers 159t

Cambridge, chancellors and vice-chancellors 146

Canada, orders and decorations 132

cancellation/postponement of a wedding 45, 115

canons 61, 138, 140t, 144t

captains 149t

cardinals, 142, 143t

cards
    admission 31
    adoption 112
    birth announcement 112-13
    business 22, 69
    correspondence 110, 113

greetings 112, 120

place cards 55

reply 31, 38

save the date 115

visiting 60-1, 68, 69

see also letters

chairmen and vice-chairmen 50, 57, 163t

Chancellor of the Exchequer 159t

chancellors and vice-chancellors 146, 147t

change of address 121

Chaplain (Honorary), to The Queen 124

chaplains (HM Forces) 140

chargés d'affaires 50

Chief Rabbis 145t

children

   of baronets/baronetesses 97t

   of knights 101

   of The Peerage 37, 83, 87t, 94, 97, 100, 101

children's thank you letters 118

chivalry, orders of 81, **98-103t**, 132

christenings, invitations to 113

Christmas cards 120

church dignitaries 50, 51, 58, 59, 60-1, 67, 101, 124, **136-45t**

Church in Wales 137

Church of England 136-40t

Church of Ireland 137

Church of Scotland 141

circuit judges 154, 155t

circulars from business mobiles 17

City of London, sheriffs 161

civic councillors 50, 163

civil partnerships 107

   see also commitment ceremonies

clergy 50, 51, 58, 59, 60-1, 67, 101, 124, **136-45t**

commanders (HM Forces) 148, 149t

commanders (police) 158t

commissioners, high 50, 53, 58, 153t

commissioners (police) 158t

commitment ceremonies 74

   see also civil partnerships

commodores 148, 149t, 152t

Commonwealth, orders and decorations 132

compliments slips 23

condolence, letters of 116-17

confirmations 113

congratulation, letters of 113, 115

consorts 162, 163t

constables (police) 158t

Convenors (Scotland) 162

copies ('cc') for emails 13

corporals 150

correspondence see business correspondence; social correspondence

correspondence cards 110, 113

councillors (civic) 50, 163

countesses and earls **88-9t**, 94, 95

County of Lancaster, giving the loyal toast 56

couples 53, 107

courtesy titles and styles 60, 94-5, 101, 102

crown appointments and honours 124, 125, 130-1

curtsying and bowing to the Royal Family 81

damehoods 102-3

daughters of The Peerage 83, 87t, 93t, 94

deacons and deaconesses 145

deans 138, 139t, 141

death notices 116

decorations and orders 34, 54, 55, **130-3**

degrees, university 54, 55, 124, 126, 146, 147t, **156-7**

delivery/read receipts for emails 13

dental officers (HM Forces) 149

Dental Surgeon (Honorary), to the Queen 124

deputy mayors and mayoresses 161

Deputy Prime Minister, The 159t

dinner parties 32

diplomas (medicine) 156, 157

diplomatic service 50-1, 67, 70t, **153t**
  see also politics
divorced persons 38, 60
doctorates 126, 146, 147t, 156
doctors 60, 69, 107, 124, 126, **156-7t**
dress codes 29, 34
dukes and duchesses 57, 58, **84-5t**, 94

earls and countesses **88-9t**, 94, 95
ecclesiastical dignitaries 50, 51, 58, 59, 60-1, 67,
  101, 124, **136-4t**
Edinburgh, Royal Society of 127
email (electronic mail) 12-15
enclosures
  business letters 20
  greetings cards 120
  invitations 31, 34, 38
engagements, announcements/parties 45, 114-15
  see also weddings
envelopes 30, 37, 74, 110
Episcopal Church in Scotland 137, 139t
'Esq' (Esquire), use of 55, 68

faxes 23
first communion 113
First Lady (US) 67
foreign nationals receiving honorary knighthoods 98
formal functions
  invitations/replies **28-31**, 71-2
  The Royal Family as guests 29, 34, **48-9**, 57, 81
  table and seating plans 50-2, 54
  toasts and speeches 56-9, 81
  see also informal functions
forms of address 66-70t, **78-107t**
Free Churches 145

garden parties, Royal 26

Garter, Order of the 99
gatecrashers, avoiding 31, 34
General Assembly (Church of Scotland) 141
generals (HM Forces) 151t
godparents 42
government
  local 160-3t
  Members of Parliament 51, 58, 124, 129, **159t**
governors, US states 67, 70
grace, at formal functions 56
grammar/spelling in emails/text messages 12, 16
greeting cards 112, 120
greetings
  ambassadors 153t
  American form 70t
  Armed Forces 151t, 152t
  business correspondence **14-15**, 15, 16, 18, 20,
   21, 21, 23
  HM The Queen/The Royal Family 78, 79, 80, 81
  legal profession 155t
  Members of Parliament 159t
  The Peerage 85t, 87t, 89t, 90t, 93t, 97t,101t, 103t
  police force 158
  social correspondence 111
  untitled persons 105t
  see also signing off
guardians 42
Guards' Division, The 150, 151t
guest lists 54
  see also names, listing of
guests of honour 48, 59, 72
guests, unmarried 30
guests, unnamed 37

heir apparent/presumptive 83
heiress apparent/presumptive 83
High Chancellor 154, 155t
high commissioners 50, 53, 58, **153t**

high importance/urgent flags for emails 12
high sheriffs, 161
high stewards 147t
'His/Her Excellency', use of 67, 153
HM Forces 60, 61, 68, 124, 129, 140, **148-52t**
honorary knighthoods 98
'Honourable/Honorable', use of
at formal/informal functions 37, 55
   men 94, 95
   Privy Counsellors 54, 104
   women 86, 89, 101, 102
honours and appointments (Crown) 124, 125, **130-1**
Hospital of St John Jerusalem, Order of 103
hosts and hostesses 30, 34, 57
Household Cavalry/Division 150, 151t
husbands 103

informal functions **32-7**, 71-3
  see also formal functions
invitations
  birth ceremonies 113
  engagement parties 115
  formal/official functions **28-31**, 71-2, 71, 106
  from HM The Queen and The Royal Family 26, 27
  informal/private functions **32-7**, 33, 35, 36, 72, 73, 106
  religious ceremonies 113
  replying to 26, 30-1, 37, 67, 72, 118
  weddings **38-45**, 40-3, 44, 74, 75

Jersey and Channel Islands, giving the loyal toast 56
Jewish religion 145
joint forms of address 106-7
judges 154, 155t
'Junior', use in names (US) 69
justices of the peace 124, 125
knights and knighthoods 60, **98-101t**, 154

Lady Mayoresses 162, 163t
Lancaster, County of, giving The Loyal Toast 56
lay brothers 142
law (England and Wales/Scotland) *see* legal profession
learned societies 124, 127
legal profession(England and Wales) 124, 125, 129, **154-5t**
see also police force
legal profession(Scotland) 124, 129, **154-5t**
letter writing
  business 20-1
  social 110-11, 120
letters
  of condolence 116-17
  of congratulation 112, 115
  thank you letters 26, 67, 116
  see also cards
letters after names 22, 37, 99t, 100, 102, 103, **124-9**, 146
  see also orders and decorations
lieutenants and deputy lieutenants 124, 125, 160, 161
Literature, Royal Society of 127
local government 50, 58, 59, **160-3t**
  see also Members of Parliament
London Gazette 98, 102
Lord Chief Justice of England 154, 155t
Lord High Chancellor 154, 155t
Lord Justice Clerk (Scotland) 154, 155t
Lord Justice of the Court of Appeal 154, 155t
Lord Justice General (Scotland) 154, 155t
Lord Mayors and Mayoresses 50, 58, 161, 163t
Lord Privy Seal 159
Lord Provosts (Scotland) 50, 58, 160, 162
lord-lieutenants 160, 161
Lords of Appeal in Ordinary 154, 155t
Lords of Session (Scotland) 154, 155t
Loyal Toast, The 56
luncheon parties 32

'Ma'am/Sir', use of 81, 150, 152

maiden names 43

Marine Corp (US) 68

marquesses and marchionesses **86-7t**, 94, 95

married women 60, 105t

marshals (HM Forces), 150, 152t

Master of the Rolls 154, 155t

masters degrees 126, 156

mayors and mayoresses 50, 161-2, 163t

medical officers (HM Forces) 149

medical practitioners 60, 69, 107, 124, 126, **156-7t**

Members of Parliament 51, 58, 124, 129, **159t**

see also local government

Methodist Church 145

Ministers of the Crown 51, 58, 124, 126, **159t**

'Miss/Ms', use of 105t

mobile phones, use of 16-17, 18, 19

Moderators (Church of Scotland) 141

Moderators (United Reform Church) 145

monsignors 142, 144t

'Mr/Mrs', use of 68, 69, 105t

names

  on admission cards 31

  on invitations 30, 37, 38, 43

  letters after 22, 37, 99t, 100, 102, 103,

  124-9, 146

  listing of 62-3, 125

  on place cards 55

naval officers (HM Forces) 149

Navy, Royal 129, 148, 149t

New Zealand, orders and decorations 133

non-acceptance of invitations 26

non-commissioned officers (NCOs) 150

numerals, usage in names (US) 69

Nursing Sister (Honorary), to the Queen 124

official functions

  invitations/replies **28-31**, 71-2

  The Royal Family as guests 29, 34, **48-9**, 57, 81

  table and seating plans 50-2, 52, 54

  toasts and speeches 56-9, 81

  see also private functions

Order of the Garter 99

Order of the Hospital of St John of Jerusalem 103

order of precedence

  ambassadors 50, 53, 58, 153

  Armed Forces 148, 150

  letters after names 100, 103, 124, 126,

  listing of names 62-3, 68

  The Peerage 84, 86, 88, 90, 92

  orders and decorations 124-5, 130-3

  in speeches 58-9

  on table and seating plans 48, 49, 50-1, 53

Order of the Thistle 99

orders of chivalry 81, **98-103**, 132

  see also baronets and baronetesses; The

  Peerage; The Royal Family

orders and decorations 34, 54, 55, **130-3**

  see also letters after names

Oxford, chancellors and vice-chancellors 146

Parliament, Members of 51, 58, 124, 129, **159t**

see also local government

party invitations 32, 36, 37, 72-3, 115

Peerage, The 37, 54, 55, 57, 58, 60, 63, **82-95t**, 98,

  102, 104, 125

  see also baronets and baronetesses; orders of chivalry;

  The Royal Family

Peerage, The (Scotland) 82, 85, 87, 89, 90, 93, 96

Physician (Honorary), to the Queen 124

physicians 156-7t

place cards 55

police force 158t

  see also legal profession

politics
  local government 50, 58, 59, **160-3t**
  Members of Parliament 51, 58, 124, 129, **159t**
  American 67, 68, **70t**
  see also diplomatic service
Pope, The 143t
postgraduate diplomas(medicine) 156, 157
postponement/cancellation of a wedding 45, 115
prebendaries 61, 138, 140t
precedence, order of
  ambassadors 50, 53, 58, 153
  Armed Forces 148, 150
  letters after names 100, 103, 124, 126
  listing of names 62-3, 68
  The Peerage 84, 86, 88, 90, 92
  orders and decorations 124-5, **130-2**
  in speeches 58-9
  on table and seating plans 48, 49, 50-1, 53
predictive text in text messaging 16
Presbyterian Church 141, 145
President, The (US) 67, 70t
President of the Board of Trade 159t
President of the Family Division 154, 155t
presidents, of official bodies/societies 57, 127
priests 144t
Prime Minister, The 58, 159t
priors, 144t
private functions **32-7**, 71-3
  see also official functions
Privy Counsellors 51, 54, 55, **104**, 124, 125,
  154, **159t**
professional bodies/societies 57, 124, 127, 128
professional names of women 103
professors 60, 146, 147t
provincials 142, 144t
provosts (Church of England) 138, 139t
Provosts (Scotland) 50, 58, 162
punctuation 22

Queen, HM The 26-7, 29, **48-9**, 57, 62, **78**
Queen's Counsel 125, 154
'quiet' zones (mobile phones) 17, 18

rabbis 145t
ranks (HM Forces) 140, **148-52t**
receptions (wedding) 38
regions, local government 160
religious ceremonies 113
remarriage 43, 85, 87, 89, 91, 93
reply cards 31, 38
replying to emails 13-14
replying to invitations 26, 30-1, 37, 72, 118
retinues, of Royal Family 48
retired clergymen 138, 139t
retired judges 154
retired officers (HM Forces) 148, 150, 152
ringtones (mobile phones) 18
Roman Catholic Church 59, 67, **142-44t**
Royal Academicians 124, 128
Royal Air Force 61, 129, 148, **152**
royal commands 26, 27
Royal Family, The 26, 27, 29, 34, **48-9**, 57, 62,
  78-81
  see also baronets and baronetesses; orders
  of chivalry; The Peerage
Royal garden parties 26
Royal Marines 61, 129, 149
Royal Navy 129, 148, 149t
royal societies 127

salutations
  ambassadors 153t
  American form 70t
  Armed Forces 151t, 152t
  business correspondence **14-15**, 16, 18, 20, 21, 23

HM The Queen/The Royal Family 78, 79, 80, 81

legal profession 155t

Members of Parliament 159t

The Peerage 85t, 87t, 89t, 90t, 93t, 97t, 101t, 103t

police force 158

social correspondence 111

untitled persons 105t

see also signing off

same-sex couples 107

save the date cards 115

Scotland

civic heads 50, 58, 160, 162

clergy 137, 139t, 141

learned societies 127

legal profession 124, 129, **154-5t**

The Peerage 82, 85, 87, 89, 90, 93, 96

seating and table plans 48-53, 54

second marriages 43, 85, 87, 89, 91, 93

senators (US) 68, 70t

Senior Service (Royal Navy) 148

'Senior', use in names (US) 69

sheriffs 59, 161

signatures (automatic), in emails 14

signing off

business correspondence 16, 20, 21, 23

emails 14-15

greetings cards 120

social correspondence 111

see also salutations

'Sir/Ma'am', use of 81, 150, 152

smoking at formal functions 56

social correspondence 110, 111, 120

see also business correspondence

Society of Antiquaries 127

sons, of The Peerage 83, 87t, 93t, 94

speeches and toasts 56-9, 81

spelling/grammar, in emails/text messages 12, 16

State Governors (US) 67, 70t

state ministers 51, 58, 124, 129, **159t**

stationery

business correspondence 23

invitations and replies 37, 38

letter writing 110, 118

step-parents 40, 41

stock invitation cards 32, 33

styles by office 55, 70t, **136-63t**

suffixes 55, 60, 96

Surgeon (Honorary), to The Queen 124

surgeons 156-7t

table and seating plans 48-53, 54

teleconferencing 19

text messages 16-17, 19

thank you letters 26, 67, 116, 118, 119

'The', use of in titles 63, 95

Thistle, Order of the 99

titled persons, styling of 60, **82-103t**

toasts and speeches 56-9, 81

United Reform Church of England and Wales 145

university degrees 54, 55, 124, 126, 146, 147t, **156-7**

unmarried couples 107

unmarried guests 30

unmarried women 105t

unnamed guests 37

untitled persons 55, 63, **105t**

urgent/high importance flags for emails 12

vice admirals 148, 149t

vice-chancellors 146, 147t

Vice-President (US) 70t

vice-presidents, of official bodies/societies 57

video conferencing 19

viscounts and viscountesses **90-1t**, 94, 95

visiting cards **60-1**, 71

voicemail 18
Volunteer Reserve (RAF) 152

weddings
  announcements 115
  guest lists 54
  invitations to **38-45**, 74, 75
  postponements and cancellations 45, 115
  receptions 38, 43
  thank you letters 118
  see also engagements
wives, former wives and widows 60, 69
  of baronets 96, 97t
  of barons 92, 93t
  of clergy 101
  of dukes 84, 85t
  of earls 88-9, 89t
  of knights 100, 101
  of marquesses 86, 86t, 87t
  of mayors 163
  of a peer by courtesy 95
  of Provosts (Scotland) 162
  remarriage 43
  of viscounts 90-1t
women
  ambassadors 153
  clergy 145
  damehoods 102-3
  divorced 60
  Lady Mayoresses 162, 163t
  married, 60, 105t
  peers 82, 83
  presidents 57
  Privy Counsellors 104
  professional names 103
  unmarried 105t
Writers to the Signet (WS) 124, 129
writing paper 110